MY APPALACHIAN TRIAL II

CREAKING GEEZER, HIDDEN FLAGON

Steve Adams

My Appalachian Trial II: Creaking Geezer, Hidden Flagon

by

Steve Adams

Copyright © 2016 by Steve Adams. All rights reserved. Reproduction in whole or part of this publication without express written consent is strictly prohibited.

Please visit:

www.steveadams.info

About the Author

It took me over 40 years in the insurance industry to come to the conclusion that life could—and should—be better. I decided that climbing mountains, walking through forests, living like a hobo, then writing about my experiences would be a lot more fun.  The publication of these two volumes has taken a lot of time, energy, and self-examination that I have enjoyed immensely. Added to that enjoyment is the realization that I can articulate my thoughts and put them into these pages. My writing career is in its early stages and I hope that you want to join me in this and other adventures in the future.

As always, my lovely wife, Diane, will be with me every step of the way at our home in sunny Florida.

Acknowledgments

Any book, however intimate, is a collaborative process. When I was writing, I was entirely responsible for everything that appeared on my laptop. Once those long, lonely days were over, the true job of a writer came into focus. I canvassed several friends, listened to countless podcasts, and read innumerable articles about the current state of the publishing industry.

All the advice I received led me to the need for a serious, professional editor and a book cover designer. My editor—suggested by a fellow hiker and author—was Liz Coursen. She introduced me to the concept of American English. This was a concept that I initially resisted. However, as I progressed through the editing process, a lot of it made sense and I buckled under her pressure. I believe, and I hope, that Liz has helped make this a better read than it was. Any remaining mistakes are mine, as is the occasional bad language.

I had the title in my head from the very beginning, although it was originally intended to be just one book. Consequently, the decision to split it into two volumes meant that I needed something other than "I" and "II" as differentiators. In this social media world, I naturally turned to Facebook to enlist help in coming up with sub-titles. I couldn't have been more delighted when my son, Rob, suggested those chosen.

I really love the covers of these two books, so additional thanks goes to Wootikom Hanroog. He understood what I wanted and patiently altered the design until I was happy. I found him through 99Designs, so kudos to them.

Two last shout-outs. First, the Appalachian Trail Class of 2014. I met many people on this journey, very few of whom I would have met had we not been dreamers. I've mentioned some and left out others, but there wasn't a single person I met who didn't have some impact upon my hike. Most of this impact was beneficial, though I'm sure that, even now, we are all still working out what this has meant to us. In some ways, I hope we never find out and retain that magic.

Last—but certainly most—I want to thank Diane for leaving me to pursue not only my hiking dream but also my writing dream when I returned home. I hope that I have made her proud of me.

Steve Adams
April 2016

This book is dedicated to my wife, Diane. I never needed her permission to take this trip, but I always needed her buy-in. There is a significant difference, and I will forever be grateful to her for understanding that.

Contents

Chapter 1: Back into it 1
Chapter 2: Putting in the miles 11
Chapter 3: Billy Goat 19
Chapter 4: Waynesboro to Elkton 33
Chapter 5: More Shenandoah 45
Chapter 6: Front Royal to Harpers Ferry 57
Chapter 7: Harpers Ferry to Pennsylvania 67
Chapter 8: Welcome to Pennsylvania 77
Chapter 9: Hitting the rocks 89
Chapter 10: More rocks and more people 101
Chapter 11: Into Palmerton 113
Chapter 12: Leaving Pennsylvania 123
Chapter 13: New Jersey 133
Chapter 14: Into New York 145
Chapter 15: Out of New York 157
Chapter 16: Connecticut 167
Chapter 17: Massachusetts 175
Chapter 18: The mountains start again 185
Chapter 19: Vermont 195
Chapter 20: Killington and beyond 205
Chapter 21: Into New Hampshire 217
Chapter 22: The Whites and the Presidentials 227
Chapter 23: Out of New Hampshire 245
Chapter 24: Into Maine 255

Chapter 25: More mountains 265
Chapter 26: Monson and slackpacking 277
Chapter 27: Last miles 287
Chapter 28: Katahdin and beyond 297
A Call to Action 313
Continue the Journey 314
One last thing 315

Chapter 1: Back into it

The return flight to Roanoke was filled with thoughts of Diane, and our marriage. We had tried our best, but I knew that we were concerned, both in terms of the next few months on the trail, and what lay beyond. My antibiotics had meant a cessation of any drinking activity, so I couldn't even have a beer on the plane to make myself feel better. The course of pills was almost at an end, my leg was entirely healed, and my head was turning to thoughts of the trail. By the time I touched down in Roanoke, I was raring to go.

My Appalachian Trial II: Creaking Geezer, Hidden Flagon

My initial plan had been to hike four or five miles, then set up camp short of McAfee Knob, the most famous vista on the Appalachian Trail. However, once I was on the plane, I decided to ease back into the trip, leaving my first hike until Friday morning. In this way, I was able to return to Joe and Donna's hostel at Four Pines, mount an assault on the Homeplace for a third time, then sleep the night in my tent in their field.

Joe and Donna were a little surprised to see me and, after explanations and introductions, I met my new fellow hikers. Virtually everybody I had met to this point had been friendly. This bunch was no exception, so we all headed out to the restaurant as a band of brothers and sisters. The characters on the A.T. may have changed, but the character never did.

Returning from another stupendous blowout, I decided not to go straight to bed. Instead, I took another shot at cornhole. Priding myself on my competitive spirit—and entirely ignoring my previously abysmal form—I was confident that I'd soon be teaching these southern boys and girls a thing or two about the game. I lobbed a few bags, and was ready to take on all comers. Bama, a young, ex-military girl from Alabama said she had played a bit, so I smiled and got ready for the slaughter of the innocent.

Unfortunately, the innocent turned out to be me. My five-foot-nothing opponent totally wiped the floor with me, 21-0, 21-4. The fact that she was then convincingly beaten by a young guy straight after, confirmed to me that, perhaps, cornhole wasn't my game. I resumed my position as spectator.

There were chickens roaming about Joe's farm, and my tent was situated perilously close to a barn that they all seemed quite keen on. Unfortunately, the rooster was a somewhat showy character. He appeared to be operating on U.K. time, making a dreadful noise at 2:30 in the morning, or 7:30 in the U.K. The fact that his favorite spot, once he was outside the barn, turned out to be directly outside my tent, didn't do a lot for me. I woke with a start, then was forced to listen to him going on for about another twenty minutes before shoving a cork in it.

Fortunately, I was able to fall back to sleep, then was woken by my alarm at 5:30. I had set it this early to really get to grips with my slightly increased mileage requirement of 13.3 miles a day. It still took me two hours to get myself sorted out, so I was heading down the road, back to the trailhead, by 7:30.

I was nervous about my return. My legs were a touch shaky at first, although I made good progress for the first mile or so. Very early on, there was a delightful walk through another meadow. I started to feel comfortable once more, relaxing and getting myself back into the flow. I must have relaxed a touch too much, because, just after I'd passed the 700-mile marker, I very nearly stepped on a black snake. I had seen plenty of black snakes by this point, yet this fellow was about five feet long and reared up in front of me. He also didn't seem inclined to let me through. Once more, I gave way to the rightful owner of the path, skirted him judiciously, and went on my way.

Just two hours into my day, I had done five miles. I was feeling a bit complacent about how easy my 13.3 mile target was going to be, when I realized that I was lost. I'm not entirely sure how it happened, but I was suddenly going down a wide road that didn't seem quite right. After about a third of a mile, I spotted an information board ahead of me. There was a map that showed me that I was plugging away down a fire road. The A.T. was running parallel, but a few hundred yards away in the woods. The two roads were due to intersect about two miles ahead. It just didn't seem right to walk on until I got back on track, so I simply turned around and retraced my steps. What else was there to do? Sometimes, my British sense of what is right really pisses me off.

As a reward for doing the right thing, this slight hiccup turned out to be fortuitous. I ran into a really friendly guy named Tim. He was out for a day hike up to McAfee Knob, the most photographed landmark on the entire trail. As I've noted before, hiking the Appalachian Trail could be a solitary endeavor. Although I got together with people most evenings, I was often entirely by myself for a lot of the day. As a consequence, when I did happen to run into somebody with whom I could have a decent conversation, it was nice to team up, if only for the short time that we spent together.

Tim was very laid back, and we chatted back and forth all the way up to McAfee Knob. For me, it actually made the hike easier, which was another advantage of teaming up from time to time. The fact that I wasn't struggling to keep up with him also helped. I realized that my hiking legs were still intact, despite the enforced layoff.

At the top, quite apart from the iconic nature of the shot, I was staggered once more by the scope of my view. The Knob boasts an enormous panorama of the Catawba Valley and North Mountain to the west, Tinker Cliffs to the north, and the Roanoke Valley to the east. While these may be the facts, from where I stood I felt as if I was seeing the whole world laid out in front of me into the infinite distance. I felt gratitude once more to have had the opportunity to get back to my adventure.

Tim and I took turns at capturing the money shot with each other's camera. I often look back at the one he took of me.

It is a little misleading, however, because the camera records the solitude of the hiker, as well as the inspiring view that he has. In my case, the solitude was more than a touch disturbed by a couple of jabbering Japanese girls about ten feet behind me. They were eating sandwiches, though chewing didn't seem to interrupt the flow of their relentless conversation.

Sometimes, things aren't quite as they seem. The cropping facility on my iPhone gave me the picture I wanted, as opposed to the one that Tim took.

This seemed as good a place as any to stop, so we sat on a nearby rock, then tucked into lunch in a moment of quiet, but companionable contemplation.

I was sorry to see Tim head back the way we had come, for we had bonded in that short period of time we had hiked together. I reflected once more about the nature of relationships on the trail. I started to hope that I'd eventually be able to share some of the adventure, as opposed to going the remaining 1,500 miles on my own.

I had set a 16-mile target for the day, so I wistfully left MacAfee Knob behind. I soon ran into a trail maintainer, no more than 400 yards from the top. These guys are amazing. Some people see it as their duty to maintain this great trail for others. They simply get up there, and get on with it, for no other reward than helping people to enjoy their hike. This particular guy was lopping off branches just to make my day easier. I thanked him for the work he was doing and continued on my way.

I'd only covered another 100 yards when I heard a huge commotion in the trees just ahead of me. I couldn't imagine anything other than a bear that would make so much noise. I cautiously moved forward, ready to run as I turned each corner. They say that you shouldn't do that. The correct method is not to engage the bear, backing up quietly and slowly without making eye contact. While I entirely understood the theory, I couldn't imagine doing anything other than screaming like a girl, dropping my backpack, and running as if I was being chased by Lucifer himself. My first meeting with a bear was still a ways off, and, as the forest fell silent once more, I was grateful for the delayed introduction.

Thinking that my day for wonderful views was done, I had an extra treat a few miles further on. After a couple of miles dipping down and through Brickey's Gap, the path rose again. It took me up to the extraordinary Tinker Cliffs, which I had spotted from MacAfee Knob. While the Knob was all about one rock and the view, the Cliffs were doubly spectacular, with great views and a sensational walk. The path trailed all the way along the top of the Cliffs for about half a mile, sometimes enticingly—and perilously—close to the edge. If McAfee Knob gets all the attention, then Tinker Cliffs is the unacknowledged gem. Apart from the money-shot picture, I'd take Tinker Cliffs every time.

I was getting tired now, and accepted that I'd probably over-reached for this first day back. Pushing through the tiredness, I eventually reached Lambert Meadow Shelter, where I spent the evening chatting with a group of weekend hikers while we sat around eating. There was an excellent camping spot across the river, so I set up there. My only neighbor for the night was a very quiet young man, Bilbo. Apparently, he had hairy feet and was fairly short, so he was named after a hobbit. Once more, I wondered why on earth some people didn't choose their name before setting out.

My Appalachian Trial II: Creaking Geezer, Hidden Flagon

Having committed to more mileage, it made sense to retain my 5:30 alarm call because I was pushing for 20 miles the following day. A bunch of idiots had come into camp at about midnight, and, unusually, made a hell of a racket, so sleep was a bit of a non-issue. Consequently, the alarm was more a courtesy than anything else, but I was still one of the last to leave. It was 8 o'clock this time, and I wondered again where the two-and-a-half hours had gone.

I really attacked the early miles. After a couple of hours, I was merrily munching on a Snickers without a care in the world. That turned out to be the high point of the day. While I sat there, my legs noticeably set, as if to concrete. Once I got going again, I was a different hiker. I became sluggish, with no pep. It was the only time that a Snickers had no discernible beneficial effect upon me.

I spoke to Diane about it and she reminded me that the antibiotics were strong and doubtless remained in my system. The blood work had also shown that I had a touch of anemia, so that may have been another reason for the sudden weakness. Also, maybe the 11-day break had taken more of a toll than I thought. Whatever it was, I didn't feel at all good. I decided to take a short break at Daleville. I ran into Bama, my cornhole nemesis, and she told me that there were restaurants in Daleville, only a short walk from the trail. The thought of pizza drove me forward. Sure enough, like a mirage, Pizza Hut appeared miraculously through the trees, just before I emerged onto the road. I've been fortunate enough to have eaten in some of the finest restaurants in the world, but seeing Pizza Hut materializing in the forest that day was every bit as exciting as eating at Jules Verne, the dazzling restaurant located a third of the way up the Eiffel Tower. Context is everything, as I'd repeatedly been reminded.

A large meat-lovers pizza and two Buds later, I was hoping that I'd be revived, ready for another half-a-dozen miles at least. It was then that I made the fatal error of spotting a cheap motel next door, and the prospect of a snooze became more of an attraction. I checked in, showered, and laundered, then slept for a couple of hours. When I woke, I gulped down nearly two liters of water, so I may also have been insufficiently hydrated.

My plan had been to get back up to 20-mile days straightaway, but I revised that to a more realistic target of 15-milers for the next few days at least. I even wondered if I was going through the infamous Virginia Blues, though I quickly ditched that idea. On further reflection, I'd probably underestimated how much my break at home had affected me. That night, I slept well, with a new, slightly more modest goal, thrilled to be back on the A.T.

Chapter 2: Putting in the miles

As I often did, I berated myself over my short day and stopover in Daleville. I was serious about my new target mileage, but felt that I'd let myself down by finishing the day after less than ten miles. I was trying to be realistic about my likely progress in the later, more mountainous states of Maine and New Hampshire. I knew that to get somewhere close to my 13.3-mile average for the rest of the trip, I needed to be pushing out 20-mile days in Virginia, as often as possible.

The first mile or two out of Daleville was simple enough. The trail crossed a couple of intersecting roads before starting to climb for just shy of four miles up to Fullhardt Knob Shelter. I took the opportunity for a break, and an examination of its rather elaborate water source. You're probably thinking, not unreasonably, "Get a life," but you'd be surprised how interesting these things can be to hikers.

The shelter collected its rain runoff through a cistern system hooked to the roof. It then flowed through a freeze-proof valve down to a spigot, where hikers could collect their water, without trekking half a mile down a godforsaken path. The operable word in that sentence is "down," because that would always be followed by an unwelcome "up." For me, the distance to a water source from a shelter was part of the decision-making process when I was deciding where to stay. Finding a spigot attached to a shelter, providing easily collectible water, was my version of finding a $20 note on the ground and nobody nearby. Perspective is a wonderful thing.

The hike up that morning provided me with another reminder that I was sharing the trail with its more natural inhabitants.

I was now heading for the Blue Ridge Mountains, where I would come quite close to the road most of the time, often crossing it, so I wasn't expecting to see too much that was breathing and not human.

Walking along a narrow, quiet part of the trail, I came across a mother and baby deer, just in front of me. Deer normally bolted straight into the bushes, but these two simply went further on up the trail, pausing and looking back. Because I hadn't expected them to behave in this way, or hang around waiting for me, I didn't pull my camera out. They played peek-a-boo with me for about five minutes before diving into the undergrowth. It was a delightful couple of minutes.

Somewhat less delightful was another truculent black snake, which decided to set up camp right in the middle of my path, daring me to do something about it. We sort of looked at each other for a minute or two, before he slithered away, as if dismissing me rather disdainfully. I'm sure I could hear him mutter "Wuss," as he went on his way. That was a charge to which I was delighted to plead guilty.

I got to Bobblets Gap Shelter, at the end of a steep blue-blazed path, following an 18-mile day. My appearance instantly lowered the collective IQ. Everybody in the shelter had some association with chemistry, while my link with the subject was tenuous at best. There was a couple heading south on a section hike who were chemical engineers, while Rip Van Winkle was a chemistry teacher. Even Yak, who turned up soon after me, majored in chemistry in college.

Despite my clear intellectual disadvantage, we had a lively chat and a few laughs. I made sure that we stayed well away from chemistry once I'd shared the full extent of my knowledge on the subject. I recounted that I'd learned various chemical symbols for a test while at high school about 50 years ago, scoring 100 percent. Exactly what they meant or did was, and remains to this day, a total mystery to me. However, I can still remember that Au is gold and Na is sodium. I can also state with some certainty that this information has had absolutely zero impact on my life since that time, but I can't shake it from my head after all these years. Given that I now arrive in front of the refrigerator at home and have no clue as to what I'm looking for, or even doing there, shows, I think, how arbitrary memory can be.

    I tented, and had the fun of dealing with a rainy night. Despite an intense downpour, I was able to stay dry. I was pleased that my 18-and-a-half miles had more than wiped out the previous day's meager total. During the next couple of months, there were few things more satisfactory than surplus mileage.

    One of the downsides of this shelter was the hike back up the blue-blazed trail to rejoin the A.T. Fortunately, the rain had stopped in the early hours and my tent, while not dry, certainly wasn't the sopping mess I'd had to pack up on other occasions.

    The warmth was on my face once more. The sun filtered beautifully through the trees to create dynamic, gentle patterns on the path. At one point, a single, widening ray resembled the beam that teleported Spock and Captain Kirk back to the Enterprise. I took the opportunity to sit on a rock and stare at it, as it slowly drifted in front of me.

    With about ten miles under my belt by lunchtime, I crossed VA 614. Immediately on the other side of the road, there was another inviting water hole at Jennings Creek. Being a bit of a sucker for these things, I had prepared for this one when I had dressed earlier that morning. Throwing down my pack, I stripped down to my swimming trunks and ventured into the water. Naturally, it was ball-churningly freezing. I had filmed previous excursions into the water for posterity but this time I chose not to record myself. Let's face it, there are only so many ways to show a big bloke flouncing around in water.

I dried off and had lunch, then totally lost my momentum. It would often happen that I would be moving well, full of intention, then lose my impetus following a stop. This was one of those days. Having breezed through the morning, I only had the will to take myself up and over Fork Mountain. The climb took me up nearly 1,000 feet in less than two miles. Another deer sighting added whimsy to my day, as a young one crossed my path no more than ten yards in front of me. The cute fellow stuck to the normal script, though, and bolted before I could get my camera out.

The day was brightened by a lovely bit of Trail Magic. I was struggling uphill, when I saw a woman and four children hiking down. While the young mother dealt with a headstrong child, who was trying to rearrange all the rocks on the Trail—a Sisyphean task if ever there was one—an eight- or nine-year-old girl asked if I wanted an apple, while her brother rummaged in his pack for the fruit. I was immediately struck that none of the kids had access to technology. They were fully engaged with one another in this beautiful, natural setting. The kids were polite, curious, and joyful. While the mother may have had difficulties keeping four children literally on the straight and narrow, I was full of admiration for her willingness, and her wisdom, in giving them all the chance to commune with nature in such a way.

I eventually wimped out for the day by stopping at the wonderfully built Bryant Ridge Shelter. The shelter was set on a short, low ridge, at the foot of Floyd Mountain. I felt that the ascent to the top of Floyd could be best left for the following day. I always found it simple to persuade myself that a climb would be easier the next morning. That delusion was one that I was rarely able to resist.

I arrived at the shelter by 3:30, and just sat there, enjoying the sun. Yak and Naturally Hob came through, chatted for a while, then moved on. By this time, I had decided that the day was over, so I started to pull things out of my bag and read for a while. Eventually, Rip Van Winkle staggered in, followed later by Smoke and Smacky, a couple of quiet Austrians. With so few people there, and with rain threatening, Rip Van Winkle and I set up our tents under cover of the magnificent shelter. At least I was guaranteed a flat spot for the night.

I suppose the word "magnificent" is a little too strong to describe any shelter on the A.T. However, compared with some of the ones I'd seen, this was a sturdily built two-story structure, put together with a lot of care. Other shelters looked as if somebody had thrown a pile of logs from a great height, then driven in nails in random places.

Another couple from California stopped in for about 30 minutes. I gave them some Trail Magic of my own. They were out of gas for their stove, while I had a spare for emergencies. I was cooking at the time, so I handed over the one I was using, then started on my reserve. I confess that, as I was handing it over, I was already regretting my gesture. I hoped that this generosity wouldn't come back to bite me in the ass. I'm pleased to report that, in deference to karma, it didn't.

I had a bit of a culinary experiment the following morning. My normal breakfast combination—oatmeal, protein powder, and mashed fruit—lacked the last ingredient because I'd run out. I needed a touch of flavor, so I decided that I'd add my coffee to this gelatinous gunk. It probably won't come as the biggest surprise in the world that the resulting sludge tasted every bit as bad as it looked. Of course, I finished every last brown fleck, then licked my plate clean to avoid the chore of washing up.

I was being ambitious on this day. Once I'd staggered up the climb I'd left for myself overnight, there was more steady hiking over Apple Orchard Mountain. There used to be an Air Force radar base at the top and, at a height of 4,225 feet, it was the highest point I would reach for some time. In fact, it remained the highest point until I reached Mount Moosilauke in New Hampshire, still over 1,000 miles ahead. From then on, already nine miles into the hike, the rest of the day trended down to Matts Creek Shelter. I was on a 14-mile path that often took me back upwards, but which ultimately headed down to about 1,000 feet.

My guidebook told me that the rocks around Matts Creek Shelter were around 500 million years old. Such an assertion made me smile. I felt that it put a hefty dent into the Young Earth Creationists' theory that God made everything about ten thousand years ago. After that, nothing much happened until He decided to get going with Adam and Eve—over a six-day period—about four thousand years ago. I would imagine that 500-million-year-old rocks must really be inconvenient to Creationists.

Reading this back, you can see that I had some rather off-the-wall conversations with myself. No wonder I gave up on God. In retrospect, perhaps He gave up on me.

When I got to the shelter, I was pleased with the day. I had over 22 miles in the bank, or, in my terms, more than nine miles of credit. It had been my first day in excess of 20 miles, and I had done it in steadily increasing temperatures and high humidity. I was exhausted, but ultimately satisfied. I was particularly pleased with my Sawyer Squeeze. My previous water filtration system had been slow to gather water. The long day demanded many water stops and I was able to get much more to drink.

To celebrate, I had a dip in Matts Creek. After a couple of minutes, I got out, then sat on a log over the creek to dry out. Feeling refreshed, I dressed at the shelter. Yak, a ludicrously youthful guy in his late forties, called me over to see a mean-looking snake sitting on precisely the spot I'd been occupying a few minutes earlier.

I guess life is often about timing.

Chapter 3: Billy Goat

Yak had the shelter to himself, because nobody else turned up that evening. I was in my tent. The weather became increasingly muggy, so I tried to sleep on top of my quilt, inside my silk quilt liner.

I had managed to fall asleep when, at about 1:15, I woke to a distant thunderclap. I wasn't especially worried, but this turned out to be a precursor to increasingly close thunder and lightning, until the storm was right above me. The flashes of lightning were the most ferocious I'd ever seen. The accompanying rain, when it came, precluded me from racing to the shelter. As a consequence, I just had to wait it out. I spent the following 45 minutes checking with my night light to see if the tent had been breached in any way. Fortunately, apart from a few splashes, everything stayed fairly dry.

Earlier in the evening, Yak and I had joked about a flood warning notice nailed to the shelter. We had dismissed the notice on the grounds that it didn't seem possible that the creek would overflow. It turned out that the warning had been about accumulating rainfall, rather than an overflowing creek. Had the stream run through my tent in the dead of night, it would have just about made my day.

In the morning, Yak told me that a bear had been playing around in the creek during the storm. He also said that the lightning had downed a tree just behind the shelter. He'd braced himself in case it fell his way. We both reflected on how dreadful it would be to have the hike ended by a tree falling on us while we were asleep. I hadn't actually had that thought in my mind until that conversation. I thought of it every subsequent night I spent in the woods.

Thanks, Yak.

My reward for the 22-mile day was an easy, flat hike of only two miles to the James River, which I crossed via the James River Foot Bridge. Interestingly, and somewhat contrarily, it wasn't named Foot Bridge because it was a footbridge. Instead, it was named after Bill Foot, a 1987 thru-hiker who worked tirelessly in securing the existing piers, applying for grants, and bringing together various agencies to make the bridge a reality. Bill and his wife, Laurie, were sweetly referred to on the trail as the "Happy Feet." It is the longest foot-use-only bridge on the Appalachian Trail, and is a fitting tribute to a determined man.

Once I'd crossed, I was able to hitch a lift into Glasgow, where I had a mail drop from Diane waiting for me. The package came just in time. My new regime of eating like a demented man had nearly exhausted my supplies, so I was looking forward to replenishing my food bag with goodies. Diane hadn't let me down, adding more than I'd asked for. As she told me later, "there was room for a little extra in the box."

With a full pack, I decided to put off the reality of slinging 45 pounds onto my back for a few hours. I treated myself to a burger and fries in a cafe across from the post office at 10:30 in the morning. There is never a bad time to have a burger and fries when you're hiking. A coin laundry just up the road also allowed me to get some soap and water through my increasingly cruddy clothes. I didn't leave Glasgow and return to the trail until about 1:30 that afternoon.

The weather was about to welcome me back.

With my pack and belly both bulging with food, I was grateful for a very gentle start to the afternoon hike. I set an ambitious ten-mile target for the rest of the day, hoping to end at Punchbowl Shelter. Those first few miles were idyllic, with a flat, clear path that bore no indication of the climb to come. However, by the time I started moving up, the weather was closing in around me. It taunted me for the rest of the day.

A three-mile ascent to 3,000 feet was tough enough, yet I was constantly looking out to the east, for it was clearly raining heavily a few miles away in that direction. At the top of Big Rocky Row, I started to look around for a place to quickly set up camp in case the rain should reach me. There were plenty of spots that could take a tent, so I relaxed and moved on. Unfortunately, that was the last time there was even an inch of available space in the undergrowth, which closed in on me as quickly as the weather.

In minutes, I was buffeted by high winds and darker clouds. I made a decision that was surely an egregious breach of hiker etiquette. With the only clear ground right under my feet, I pulled out my tent, and set up directly on the trail. I'm afraid I just wanted to be inside. Fortunately, nobody came along and, very soon, the sun was out again. I was sitting inside my tent feeling like a bit of an idiot.

Packing up once more, I headed on. Ten minutes later, exactly the same thing happened. I laughed to myself, then set up the tent where I was. The sun came out. This time, three hikers passed by, tapping my tent with their poles, so I grunted a greeting. I was careful that it was sufficiently indistinct to avoid identification. Who was this oaf in the middle of the A.T., in the sun, and in his tent?

Passing the last high spot of the day, on top of Bluff Mountain, I ran into three guys. One of these men was in his forties, apparently hiking on his own, and named Billy Goat. We were still about two miles from the shelter, so I stopped to chat for a while. After this short break, we all made our own way down to the lovely Punchbowl Shelter, where I set up my tent for the third time that day. I was so pleased that I'd determined ease-of-set-up as a prerequisite for my tent all those months ago.

Billy Goat and I met again over breakfast in the morning, with the dampness dripping all around us. We spent much of the day hiking in the vicinity of one another. I really took to his dry character and quiet sense of humor.

There were a few early rises and falls which weren't too intense before a steeper trek up Rice Mountain left a far easier descent and flat hike for five or six miles. We came to the 800-mile marker, an elaborate combination of stones that must have taken an age to construct. Not wishing to waste the Kodak moment, we took pictures of one another behind the sign. When my wife saw my posting on Facebook, she entirely ignored the amount of work that went into setting up the marker. Instead, she homed in on my "skeletal look," as she referred to it. I'd always been able to translate her Puerto Rican hyperbole—and I knew that I wasn't skeletal—yet even I could see that my new eating regime hadn't remotely halted my spiraling weight loss. The concept of increasing my eating regimen seemed unlikely, but I resolved to give it a go.

I'd set another ambitious target but, with the dampness wearing me out, I was a very receptive listener when Billy Goat told me of a cheap hostel in Buena Vista. We were only two miles from the link road into town, so my ambitious day was shelved with alacrity.

Just short of the road there was a small rise, so I started to wind down and reflect. It had been a successful week back after my injury. I had done just over 100 miles, probably with antibiotics still working their way through my system. There had been a couple of tough days, but I had otherwise enjoyed the week. I felt that I was back into it. I was literally less than 200 yards from the road when I noted to myself that I'd not fallen since getting back on the trail. The thought had no sooner formed in my mind, when I slipped on a muddy spot, and deposited myself once more in the dirt—on my back—for fall number 11.

Bollocks.

Buena Vista proved to be a great stop, with plenty of food and a couple of beers to raise my energy level and recalibrate my enthusiasm.

The Blue Dog Art Cafe was the name of the hostel, with a number of rooms above this trendy local cafe and bunks in each. A hot shower always helped, so Billy Goat and I, along with a friendly young guy named Mookie, cleaned up, then headed out to a local Italian eatery to fill our boots with pizza and a few beers. That winning combination always helped send me into something of a coma, and so it proved on this evening. I spent the night doubtless annoying others, but otherwise oblivious to the world. I must have slept for eight or nine straight hours, then woke with an enthusiasm for hiking, food, and a pee, though not in that order.

This day turned out to be one of my favorite hiking experiences, not least because we encountered three examples of Trail Magic.

The first happened over breakfast in the Blue Dog Art Cafe. We were having our fill of eggs and bacon with a couple of lady hikers, when the owner of the cafe brought in a basket that had been donated by a group of local women. In the basket, there were items for hikers, so we were told to help ourselves. I chose a pack of hand wipes, which were always useful on this bacteria-overload of a trip.

We were in no hurry to get away, because the shuttle to take us back to the trail wasn't leaving until 10 o'clock. Billy Goat and I chatted with each other over coffee and breakfast, and I got to know a bit more about my new friend.

He was a very modest, thoughtful man. He was also a real-life hero, despite his protestations, as an ER doctor in San Francisco. While we were sitting there, a female day hiker—who had clearly taken a fancy to him—remarked that he looked just like Colin Firth, the British actor. This amused Billy Goat and made me laugh out loud. Since I've been in the U.S., the only person I've ever been likened to is Jeb Bush. When set against Colin Firth, that is hardly in the realms of a compliment.

All hikers referred to each other by their trail names, and I didn't find out Billy Goat's real name until the following day. He was due to meet his mother and aunt at Reid's Gap at about 4 o'clock. That tied well into my plan to get into Waynesboro for the England versus Italy World Cup soccer game. I was also going to stay over for the U.S. Open Golf Championship the following day. Billy Goat offered to give me a lift, so we hiked close to each other, taking breaks together.

When we reached Reid's Gap, about 90 minutes ahead of schedule, we took the opportunity to have a snooze in a field by the road. His mother called his phone as their car pulled up. The two women emerged, and I believe it was his aunt who screamed first.

"Travis, Travis," she screeched.

I could not have been more amazed had she shouted "Oi, Fuckface" at the top of her voice. I knew that she wouldn't refer to him as Billy Goat, but Travis was a big shock. It's funny how some people simply grew into their names, and trail names certainly took the persona of each character on the trail. Billy Goat was who he was, and Billy Goat was how I would always think of him. Travis? I don't think so.

Back to Buena Vista, the day before.

Billy Goat and I had decided to aim for The Priest Shelter, more than 20 miles ahead. It was a stretch, but we felt it was accessible if we could get through the 2,000-foot climb up and over Bald Knob in the first three miles. We knew it was going to be a daunting day, and that we'd possibly be hiking the last few miles in the dark. I would never have considered it if I'd been on my own, but this was a benefit of hiking with a partner.

At the trailhead, there was another large group of hikers milling around, mainly because of a lovely gent who was handing out all sorts of goodies to us for our second Trail Magic deliciousness. I opted for the baked beans and frankfurters, despite having overdosed on breakfast back in Buena Vista. I took an apple for dessert. Two bits of Trail Magic prior to taking a step was a great omen for the day.

In my rather anal way, I then went back across the road to touch the precise point I'd ended at the previous evening, my lone gesture to walking the entire trail. That action made me an E.F.I. hiker, my friend, Naturally Hob, once said. When I asked him what that meant, he said that I felt the need, as he did, to walk "every fucking inch."

The hill I had feared was certainly tough. However, it was significantly less so because it was the first, not the last, climb of the day. The beans and breakfast may also have contributed quite a bit to it. Billy Goat, who was faster than me, had blasted ahead, and we didn't see each other for some hours.

Once at the top, I relaxed, strode out confidently, and was soon rewarded. A small deer burst out of the undergrowth in front of me, crossed my trail, and settled in the less dense bushes on the other side, only about 30 yards away me. I pulled out my phone and shot a short video of young Bambi. He looked as curious as I was. I put my phone away, and we stood and stared at each other for five minutes before he'd had enough and went on his way.

This set the scene for a joyous day that next led me through a couple of glorious balds. I was anxious for Diane to share the moment—as much as that was possible—so I reached her on FaceTime. I thought the bald was at an end, because the path entered a narrow gap, only to emerge onto another gorgeous, even larger bald that took my breath away once more.

I'm aware that I'm boyishly enthusiastic about these things, but I never tired of seeing them.

I was hiking through open pasture and in direct sunlight for a lot of the day, so it would have been sensible to have exposed my solar charger as much as possible. Not me. I was convinced it was going to rain, so my rain cover was firmly in place in anticipation. Not for the first time, I was reminded that I suck as a weather forecaster.

The third—and most welcome—Trail Magic came after about ten miles. I had been running low on water and needed to get into my pack to get a few more protein bars, when I ran into Billy Goat and Mookie. They were looking very pleased with themselves, standing next to two coolers.

I could interpret this in two ways. First, and the most likely, they had raided the last of the coolers' contents, and were feeling smug about getting there to pick over the remnants. While I wouldn't have treated this as malicious on their part, I certainly would have been disappointed. The second possible interpretation was that there was so much food and drink in the coolers that, despite their best efforts, there was still plenty for me to raid.

It often happens that trail angels leave coolers and they were nearly always empty by the time I arrived. Using my experience to date, I was feeling confident that option one was the winner. Not this time. There was a regular cornucopia of treasures to be had, including Gatorade and real Coke, as well as Snickers bars, and other tempting morsels. I confess that I took advantage of the find, though I left tons of stuff for those who were following.

These coolers were a present from Goman, a 2012 thru-hiker. The fact that somebody thinks enough of the A.T. and its hikers that he or she is willing to stock up a cooler, then leave it to be found on the trail, is a testimony to both the camaraderie and the pay-it-forward attitude of those who inhabit this magical path.

In fading light, Billy Goat and I made it to the Priest Shelter at about 7:45 that evening, well satisfied with the mileage. For me, however, the day hadn't ended so well. A few minutes before we made the shelter, I was startled to get a call. It was news about my son Rob, and the call disturbed me for several days. He wasn't well, and I could do nothing about it. That night in the Priest Shelter was an anxious one, and I felt impotent and wretched in my tent.

For the first 800 miles on the trail I had allowed the sounds of the woods to be my company. My music and podcasts were available, but they remained largely unheard. I had been resolving my personal dilemmas, along with my futile conversations with God. I hadn't needed anything to accompany me. However, there is a limit to the amount of problems you can solve in the abstract, and I was about out of those. Along came this real-world problem about my son and I was stumped. The feeling of being completely unable to help overwhelmed me in my tent that night, and I shed a few tears.

I can't say precisely when I started listening to podcasts, audio books, and music on the trail, though I'm fairly sure that it was about this time. It also coincided with losing my connection with the trail. My loneliness, of which I'd been aware for some time, was now becoming more prominent in my mind. I don't believe that I recognized this connection at the time, yet something had distinctly shifted in my hike. I don't think that I resolved it for another 600 miles.

The Priest Shelter was just below 4,000 feet and, following a benign climb for 20 minutes the following morning, the trail traced a ridge for a mile, then rapidly descended via some steep switchbacks. We dipped from 4,000 feet to less than 1,000 feet in just four miles.

Such long descents were constantly wearing on my knees, so I had now adopted a Vitamin I regimen. I would take two ibuprofen at breakfast, followed by another two at lunchtime. This wonder drug was the ubiquitous drug of choice on the trail—along with dope, of course—and I think that it got me through some of those painful downhills. Perhaps I would have coped with them even better if I'd done the dope as well.

I spent a lot of time thinking about how Rob was doing. I was grateful, for once, for being alone. Billy Goat was ahead of me, and I struggled through the day. Not only was Rob weighing heavily on my mind but I also knew that this tough downhill would immediately be followed by another immense uphill, taking us back to almost 4,000 feet over a six-and-a-half mile stretch.

There were more spectacular views to be had from several rocky outcrops. On another day, I'm sure I would have embraced the sheer joy of the hike, yet I was down on myself. I reached the top of Three Ridges, before descending slowly to Reid's Gap, where I joined Billy Goat, soon to be unmasked as Travis.

My Appalachian Trial II: Creaking Geezer, Hidden Flagon

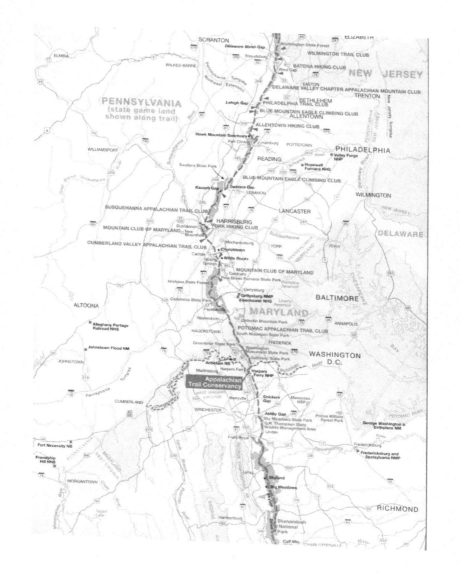

Chapter 4: Waynesboro to Elkton

Billy Goat's affable mother and aunt were especially chatty on the way into Waynesboro, and I was grateful for their uncomplicated company. I was also grateful for the distraction of the weekend. I had booked two nights in another Super 8 motel in order to scratch my latest sporting itch.

They got me there with sufficient time to check in, shower, change into some less pungent clothing, and then take a cab to the wonderful Buffalo Wild Wings, a sports bar that specialized in colossal, artery-clogging meals—sufficient for a family, but served to individuals. None of this was an issue for me, of course, and I polished off at least four portions of chicken wings, an immense slice of chocolate cake, and several beers, as I watched a disappointing defeat for England.

Back at my motel, I was able to climb into bed without setting my alarm for 5:30 the next morning. I had promised myself a luxurious lie-in. Well, as luxurious as a lie-in can be in a Super 8 motel. Consequently, it was faintly annoying when I found myself awake at precisely 5:30 the next day. The difference was that I was able to lie there on a mattress, instead of forcing myself out of bed by deflating my pad.

I treated myself to a breakfast of champions in Waffle House, a terrific franchise that offered everything I'd ever imagined an American diner to have. There were flirty, but chunky, waitresses, as well as hot coffee, with great eggs and bacon. A few grande lattes at Starbucks while I updated my blog, and I was ready for Buffalo Wild Wings once more.

Returning to a restaurant is often a disappointment, particularly if you've enjoyed it the day before. However, I can report with some delight that this wasn't the case with Buffalo Wild Wings. On this occasion, with an extended day of golf on the TV, I had to spread out my grazing over about three or four hours. I started with a fully loaded burger, washed down by a glass of beer. A short break, then I attacked the wings once more with vigor. I tried pretty much every flavor as the beers continued to flush everything on its way. With the golf winding down, as was I, I managed two slices of chocolate cake and about three cups of coffee to see out the tournament. I'd been treated to a feast of golf in a very literal sense, so I tried to walk off some of the effects by strolling a mile or so back to the Super 8.

My zero day was over. I'd spent 36 hours without talking to anybody other than waitresses and waiters. I felt ready to get back on the trail.

Much as I had enjoyed spending time in Waynesboro, I had arrived there somewhat ahead of schedule. The natural stopping off point on the trail was Rockfish Gap, right by Interstate 64, at mile 857. Billy Goat and I had been met by his mother and aunt all the way back at Reid's Gap, at mile 838. I couldn't help but feel disappointed to be effectively retracing my steps, but I knew it was necessary. I arranged for a cab to take me back.

I was setting out on a Monday morning, so, on that Sunday evening, I called for an early pick-up by a local cab company at 6:30 a.m. I made a number of phone calls from the splendor of my room at the Super 8, and was shamelessly price-gouged by various companies. The quotes ranged from $35 to $75. Happy with $35, I wondered how they could afford to do it for such a rate when others were so exorbitant.

I soon found out the next day, when nobody showed up. I had to call again. I told them that I'd been quoted a price of $35. The guy on the end of the phone did that trick that plumbers do to you when they look at your pipework: they slowly shake their head, purse their lips, then draw a deep breath between their teeth. Such a calculated action makes a noise that exhibits disbelief and imminent bad news in equal measure."I don't know where you got that number—way too low," he said.

"Your bloke gave it to me last night," I replied.

This didn't seem to fly very well. I hadn't even got to the point of my call, which was that, at whatever price, my lift for the morning hadn't appeared. When I pointed this out, he became a little more conciliatory. He told me that somebody had been booked, and that he'd make sure a cab was there within the hour.

"What about the cost?" I ventured, not wishing to leave any doubt as to what I was prepared to pay. "All right," he replied, and then hung up. I hardly had conclusive evidence that I'd gotten my way, though I felt armed with sufficient confidence that we'd agreed on 35 bucks.

My best intentions for an early start and a cheap ride had all gone to mush once more. I got everything together and headed into the parking lot. About 30 minutes later, a young guy turned up, wound his window down, and inquired, "Hiker?" This seemed to be something of a rhetorical question, given that I had shabby clothes on, was sporting a backpack, and trekking poles. "That'll be me," I responded brightly. I still wasn't entirely sure that a firm price had been agreed upon, but I was ready to argue the point.

I slung everything into the trunk and, seeing that the front passenger seat was being used as a repository for all sorts of junk, I clambered into the back. I'm not sure that this young man had been clued in to my earlier conversation on the phone but, when he heard the destination, he started going on about the cost per mile. I stopped him right there, telling him that $35 was the agreed price, and that was what I was going to pay. He thought about it for about ten seconds, clucked his tongue in an ambiguous manner, said "Okay," and then drove the rest of the way in silence. I wished that I could have that effect on London cab drivers.

The day started well, with an early discovery of a cooler that contained ice and bottles of Powerade. I helped myself to one. A few minutes later I ran into Rip Van Winkle. He was the chemistry teacher I'd met a while back at my super-smart shelter. We were roughly the same age, so we got into step, and shared much of the day chatting away. Rip Van Winkle was heading to Rockfish Gap, where he was due to be picked up by a friend. I had slightly lower ambitions, and had my sights set on the Paul C. Wolfe Shelter, making it an acceptable 15-mile day.

We had passed over Humpback Mountain—the high point of the day—before heading down a steep switchback, when we heard voices drifting up from below. Somewhat disconcertingly, these voices were many, loud, and predominately female. We looked at each other in bemusement, because the A.T. isn't generally regarded as a hotbed of female activity in such numbers. Descending further via the numerous switchbacks, the noise level increased exponentially, and we could spot the odd girl or two through the trees.

At the bottom, just short of the shelter, several girls between 13 and 15 were sitting on a log across a small stream. They were dangling their legs in the water, while others were gathering firewood for a campfire. The entire site had been overrun by what turned out to be 27 girls and three adult leaders.

Coming upon one of the hapless adults charged with keeping this estrogen-overload in order, Rip Van Winkle and I learned that they were all from the Church of Latter Day Saints. We were also informed that the girls had been instructed to keep the shelter clear for hikers.

This would have been helpful, had I been looking to spend the night in the shelter. To me, however, it was useless, for there wasn't a single spot in which to pitch my tent. While I'm all for the concept of getting kids into the woods and hiking, 30 people together at one place is simply too many to allow others to enjoy the site at the same time. We didn't express this thought to the leader. He was a rather earnest fellow who looked as if he'd be offended by any hint of criticism. Rip Van Winkle was planning to finish at Rockfish Gap, so we just waved goodbye to the Latter Day Saints, and trekked on for another five miles.

We had now been joined by Aussie, an ex-pat Australian who lived in the U.S. He had arrived at the camp just after us, and had already hiked 22 miles for the day. He looked completely out for the count, and spent the next five miles moaning quietly in pain.

Rip Van Winkle's friend and her daughter were waiting for him. We chatted a while and, having already spent a few days—and too much money—in Waynesboro, I was looking for somewhere cheap and local to spend the night before hitting Shenandoah National Park the following morning.

Nowhere was immediately apparent, despite the highway, but I spotted The Inn at Afton, perched high on top of a nearby hill. Rip Van Winkle's friend saved me another trudge by dropping me there. Once she had left me at the entrance, I waved goodbye, before looking around. There was a magnificent view across a valley and I hoped I'd found a hidden gem.

I hadn't. The place was dreadful in so many ways. Remember, I'd slept in places that previously I wouldn't have imagined were even habitable. This place was charging me money to do without many of the things that hikers took for granted at a stop. There was no access to laundry, no Wi-Fi, no food—either on-site or nearby—and the room I was given was disgusting. It may very well be that my room was the only one in this state. However, the peeling wallpaper and crumbling furniture, which exhibited generous termite occupancy, suggested otherwise. I couldn't begin to work out what the original color of the carpet had once been.

Having cast the dice, I sat on the bed for ten minutes, wondering what I could do. I needed to at least see if there was a viable alternative to this dump within a reasonable distance. Recognizing that I could be jumping out of the frying pan into an inferno, I took the chance and booked a room. I did this after I'd managed to get a refund from the amenable young woman at reception. She sounded as if I wasn't the first person to complain. She handed me back my payment without a problem, though with some resignation.

I hadn't actually planned how I was going to get to my new resting place, so I started to walk back downhill. I'd reached the bottom when an off-duty police officer kindly stopped and asked if I needed a lift. The pathetic-homeless look was really kicking in by now. When I told him where I wanted to go, he said "That's even worse than where you've just come from."This seemed hardly conceivable, yet it turned out to be a close-run thing.

Wi-Fi and laundry were the big bonuses of the Colony House Motel, though the rooms were equally awful, with the food opportunities similarly non-existent. That said, I was able to speak with Diane and launder my clothes, so I felt that I was ahead of the game. If you ever happen to find yourself at Rockfish Gap, I strongly suggest you don't sleep local. Swallow the extra expense of Waynesboro and thank me later.

Again, you're welcome.

For me, as a transplanted Brit, Shenandoah conjured images of westerns from the 1950s. The heroes were hardy, silent types, overcoming nasty incursions by what Americans now refer to—without any hint of irony—as Native Americans. Having fought back the pesky Red Indians, our hero would then find true love with a ludicrously good-looking woman, who looked as out of place in a shack as a bacon sandwich at a bar mitzvah.

As a consequence, I put my pack together the following morning with a rare anticipation of the excitement ahead. Shenandoah was famous for its bears. For me, bears were like the pot of gold at the end of the rainbow, and I wasn't getting the gold right now. Nonetheless, when I set out I was full of excitement about what lay ahead. I soon left the road and headed back into the woods.

My first impression of the park was that it was scruffy and unkempt. While I enjoyed the green tunnel, it was normally accompanied by a well-maintained path. The path in these early miles often had branches touching from either side, and I was disappointed at how neglected the trail was. Listen to me, complaining that nobody had taken the time to clear a path for me, as if it were my right. Of course, I soon shook that ungrateful thought from my mind and got on with it, delighted to be hiking at a brisk pace and emerging regularly into the open.

The sun was cranking up now in Virginia. It was the middle of June, and my sweat glands responded with their customary enthusiasm. I was drenched within thirty minutes. While that became uncomfortable, I started to enjoy the relatively gentle paths that made up my day. The trail would intermittently cross Skyline Drive, providing views for both drivers and hikers across the valley below and to the hills beyond. Those views from the road were among the best that I saw in the park. I was always amused to see cars drive up to an overlook—called a lay-by in the U.K.—wind down their window, stick a camera out of the car, click, and then drive on. Nine out of ten drivers would act in this way. I conceded that I, too, would probably have been inclined to do the same had I been driving. As a hiker, now inured to the pace of things on the trail, I always sat and contemplated the view, often taking the opportunity to have a short snack to assist my contemplation.

I was ready for the day to end by the time I got to the bottom of the hill leading up to the blue blaze that took hikers to Blackrock Hut. I'd completed a second straight day of 20 miles and was ready for some rest, yet this was the sharpest climb of the day. The heat was intense as I pushed forward. Just before the turn off, I heard what I instantly thought were footsteps running up behind me. In that moment, as I turned, I expected to see a wild bear make a lunge for my throat. There was nothing. Having stopped suddenly, I looked around for the source of the pounding. It was me. The sound I'd heard was my own heartbeat. This was reassuring and alarming in equal measure. I sat on a nearby rock and waited for normal service to resume, before slowly heading into camp for the night.

I spent some of the evening over dinner chatting to an engaging young woman, Amber, whose husband was a military man. He had served seven terms in Iraq and Afghanistan. It's always a bit of a lottery to ask the obvious question, but I went ahead and asked if he'd gotten through it okay. She smiled and said that it had been fine. He'd been shot several times although nothing too serious. Her equanimity was alarming, and all of us at the table expressed our amazement at how military families seem to take such life-and-death times in their stride. Amber shrugged and responded, "What else can you do?" There seemed to be nothing more to say, yet the raised eyebrows around the table told their own story.

The early morning climb the next day soon landed us near the top of Blackrock. There was a collection of massive boulders beside the trail to scramble up and take in the panoramic views below. Amber and I stopped for a Snickers and a few pictures, while another splendid day unfolded in front of us.

I was setting my sights slightly lower on this day because I'd read about the various waysides in the park and I very much wanted to visit them. These were cafes along the route of Skyline Drive, disappointingly far from where the A.T. crossed the drive itself, so extra effort was required to get to them. My fellow hikers and I thought that this was to discourage us and to encourage those with normal appetites. The cafe owners obviously didn't factor in the desire of hikers for food other than ramen noodles.

There was a half-mile detour downhill to reach the Loft Mountain Wayside. We would have a steep half-mile climb back uphill afterwards, but Amber and I, along with a young lad named Gator, took the plunge. Following another relentless assault upon our stomachs, we all dozed off in the afternoon sun on the grass outside, as drivers pulled up and waddled past us into the wayside.

I'd been hearing reports from my fellow travelers that bears were around. Indeed, when I woke from my doze, one of the day trippers was telling anybody who wanted to hear that she had just spotted a bear near the wayside. It felt like there were at least 100 bears to every person in the park, although they were all studiously avoiding me. It was becoming almost embarrassing.

Another gasping climb back to the trail and I was away again, leaving Amber making slightly slower progress. I stopped for a break about an hour later and she caught up to me. She commented that I must attract animals as I pass through. To my quizzical look, she said "Didn't you see the two piles of bear..." she hesitated, "....excrement back there?" She had decided upon *le mot juste*, and it was certainly the first time I'd heard bear shit referred to in such elegant terms. "A bear was right next to the first pile, only ten feet into the bushes." I'd missed it again, as I did later in camp, at Pinefield Hut, when somebody called out that a bear was on the hillside overlooking our site. Already snuggled down in my quilt, I shrugged and turned over. If it wasn't meant to be, then that was okay. But I didn't have to wait much longer, and when it happened, it was worth the wait.

Chapter 5: More Shenandoah

I had arranged a food drop from Diane for the following day, in Elkton. That meant a short 11-mile day, though there were considerable climbs to keep my attention. Crossing Hightop Mountain—my sharpest climb of the day—also allowed me to pass the 900-mile mark.

I had an ulterior motive at the back of my mind, for I was hoping to take in the soccer World Cup match between England and Uruguay on a TV somewhere. Quite where I was going to watch the game hadn't actually suggested itself as yet, though I was confident that I could turn on sufficient British charm somewhere or other. While on the trail, I always kept an eye on the sporting fixtures coming up. I tried to find myself in a town when one of the major golf tournaments or an England World Cup match was showing on TV.

I was relaxed by now about my ability to hitch a lift. Back on Skyline Drive once more, I stuck out my thumb for only a few minutes before a friendly truck driver pulled over and welcomed me into his cab. As usual, even though there are hundreds of hikers doing the A.T. every year, my new friend was fascinated by the task I was undertaking. He quizzed me about my motivation. He was also in his early sixties, and got a real kick about the fact that I was hiking the whole trail at that age. He said he'd never be able to do it, even though he was physically fit and of average weight. I reversed roles in my head and thought I'd probably have trotted out the same denial had I picked him up. How far I had come in a few months.

He wanted to know how I was recording my adventures, so I told him about my blog. Having concluded that he'd never be able to do it himself, he said he'd walk it vicariously through me. I don't know if he did read the blog, but I do know that assuming you can't do something is 90 percent of the way to doing nothing.

He dropped me at a Mexican restaurant. I asked for a booth and piled my pack and poles on the seat opposite, then set about demolishing guacamole, fajitas, nachos, tacos, and a couple of beers, while working out how to watch the game.

I asked my server if he was a soccer fan and he responded enthusiastically. However, he noted quickly that the various TVs mounted through the restaurant didn't carry ESPN, the U.S. carrier for the competition. This was an unwelcome hitch, so I asked if they had Wi-Fi in the restaurant. He told me that his boss had a private account, but that it wasn't shared with the public. I must have pulled the pathetic-loser look once more, explaining that I had an iPad, and that if I could attach to his boss's system, I could keep him up-to-date with the score of the big game. You had to be there to appreciate how well this worked. The young man was suddenly motivated. Within five minutes, I was moved to a booth as close as possible to the modem, my tablet was plugged into a convenient power point, and my new friend brought me a complimentary beer, more nachos, and a bowl of salsa. The story should have had a perfect ending, with a convincing win by England. Sadly, life isn't like that, and the country of my birth was out of the World Cup. After the game, I thanked my friend, packed away my iPad, and found a cheap motel nearby.

The motel owner returned me and a couple of section hikers to the trail at 7 o'clock the following morning. I set off in high spirits on another beautiful, crisp day.

The early hike took me along the edge of the forest, on a footpath through a meadow. I hadn't been hiking for more than about thirty minutes when I heard a noise to my right. The path had now gone back deep into the woods. I stopped and peered through the trees to where I thought the sound came from. I saw a mass of black at the top of a tree, and suspected that this could be my first bear sighting. I held my breath. My immediate thought was one of excitement, followed instantly by one of fear."Could this be it?" I whispered to myself, pulling my camera phone from my pocket. I still didn't know what it was, if anything, when the noise started up again. The black mass was on the move. I was now hoping it really *was* a bear, as anything else that size would have given me a bloody heart attack.

While this probably lasted no more than 15 seconds, the whole thing unraveled slowly as I took it all in. The downward movement of whatever it was made me switch from photo to video on my phone. I was rewarded as a large bear dropped heavily to the ground, and, thankfully, made off in the opposite direction. That alone would have been wonderful, yet there was further noise. No more than two seconds later, another, much smaller, bear appeared, following the first. Still another came out of the same tree a second later. A fourth dropped from the next tree, and all four scampered away deeper into the forest. It looked like a mass prison breakout.

I was ecstatic, having gone from zero bears to four in about ten seconds. Anxious for cell coverage to tell Diane, I was able to get through to her about twenty minutes later. In the interim, I had chalked up another deer on the trail. There was quite the menagerie to tell her about. I called her excitedly while preparing to fill my water bottle at a stream. As I finished the call, I stooped to fill my bottle. I was just rising from the stream when a fifth bear—bigger than the others—emerged from the bushes no more than 20 yards ahead of me, directly onto the trail. Happily, it ignored me and waddled ten yards down the path before heading back into the forest. My wet hands prevented me from getting my camera out, though I'd seen five bears in 20 minutes, and even had film of four of them.

The Appalachian Trail had deigned to show me its goodies all in one go, for which I was grateful. I was also aware that my fear of these creatures had been misplaced. Like the snakes before them, they wanted nothing to do with me, and, if left alone, would certainly allow me to share their forest.

There was another deer at Bearfence Hut, where I stopped for lunch. This one seemed to have no fear, coming within feet of me while I talked to it, though I was wary of getting too close. I'd been warned of the presence of deer ticks, and had found a couple on me in recent days. Fortunately, none had embedded themselves in my skin, though constant checks helped with that. Lyme disease was an affliction that I wanted to avoid at all costs. Several experienced hikers had told me that ticks on the trail were infinitely more dangerous than bears.

It had been an exhilarating day. I was keenly aware that I'd been on my own for most of the day, and that I'd been unable to share my excitement with anybody, apart from my call to Diane earlier. I'd spent a few evenings camping around a number of guys in their 20s and 30s—Nobody, Lumberjack, Doctor, and Tomahawk—but they were now ahead of me. I was unlikely to see them again unless they slowed down. I was just thinking about them when they paraded, like a truncated version of Snow White's dwarfs, away from my destination for the night, Big Meadows Campsite. They had called in for a shower, but were now moving on. I, not wishing to appear so needy, waved them past me. Sometimes my British reserve totally ticks me off.

Big Meadows was a great spot. There was a lodge for food and drink, five-minute showers for a quarter, and a coin laundry. I was trying to find where to pitch my tent when I was approached by a lady who turned out to be the camp host, Eileen. She seemed to take a liking to my accent, and generously allowed me to camp for free in her spot, next to where she and her husband had parked their RV.

At the lodge, I took in another World Cup match, along with a burger and a glass of wine, after a shower and laundry. I had enjoyed the day, but was now becoming lonely for longer periods. I turned in that night listening to music on my iPhone, further exacerbating my sense of isolation. I knew I could go home at any time, but I also knew that I'd never forgive myself for quitting out of loneliness. I already had the picture at MacAfee Knob, though the one that I wanted above all others was the shot at the top of Katahdin. It became an obsession in the coming weeks and months that I couldn't shake, with each iteration of the photograph in my mind looking better than the previous one. While I knew that for all of us on the trail it was about the journey, I became aware at this time that it was also going to be about the destination. This feeling became more pronounced as the miles mounted.

Not only did Eileen allow me to camp for free, she also became my provider and savior the following morning. I was sitting next to my tent, having boiled water for coffee and oatmeal, when she emerged from the RV bearing gifts. There was a banana, which was scrumptious, along with a cup of real coffee, which was sublime. We chatted for a while. I told her that I'd been checking for ticks and that I'd found five on me the previous evening while preparing for bed. She returned to her RV and came out with a half-full can of OFF! "Spray this every day below knee level, under and over your pants, and make sure you spray your boots. You'll never have another tick." Extraordinarily, I never saw another one for the rest of my time on the trail, and I followed these instructions every day. Who knew?

I planned a 19-mile day for that Saturday. I chose to ignore Luray, which was a regular stopping point for most, and pushed on to Pass Mountain Hut. It was immediately apparent that the weather was about to deteriorate, with the clouds drifting in and filling the valley below. While this was an ominous sign, it was always a delight to me that I was hiking above the clouds, yet I knew that the day was going to be more difficult than of late.

I had another restaurant in mind for that day, Skyland. It was originally a nineteenth-century summer resort owned by an Appalachian Trail pioneer, George Freeman Pollock. With more than a touch of irony, Pollock was eventually forced to sell and give up management of the resort, having pushed hard in earlier times to evict surrounding small landholders to create a national park. I suppose you reap what you sow. Whatever its antecedents, Skyland was a grand summer home and I pitched up in anticipation of another stupendous blowout.

I'd become used to being shuffled into the corner of restaurants and, to be frank, I could quite understand. When you have two competing constituencies, it makes sense to separate the ones with personal hygiene issues, and I certainly fell into that category. Fortunately, I'd been able to come to terms with my second-class-citizen status, so I couldn't care less where they put me.

One thing in which the management was distinctly egalitarian, however, was in its collection of my cash. In quick order, I woofed down some chowder, mangled an enormous burger, then demolished the house specialty (a baked ice cream pie) after the inevitable "Have you left enough room for dessert?" question had been asked. The whole lot must have added up to at least 2,500 calories. My newfound power allowed me to breeze through the afternoon session with renewed vigor. The hike was often a case of calories in and calories out; Shenandoah was helping with the calories in.

Bear number six was the highlight of my afternoon, as I caught up with Lumberjack, who was involved in a Mexican standoff with a reluctant bear on the trail. Lumberjack had taken to wearing a lilac lacrosse shirt with a dubious provenance: he claimed it was from a girls' high school team. Precisely how he obtained it, I couldn't tell you. While I wasn't exactly Beau Brummel on the trail, this was one of the stranger outfits I saw.

The shirt—more of a crop top—revealed quite an expanse of his hairy stomach, being about eight sizes too small.

The bear had no interest in moving, while Lumberjack and I had no intention of forcing the issue, so we sat there for a while. Eventually, the bear pushed off, and we all went on our way. The lack of any need to be in a particular place was a great thing to draw upon when I had to sit and wait anywhere. I've retained this feeling since I returned from the trail.

By now, the rain that had threatened earlier started to make good on the threat, and I quickly became substantially soaked. As always, there was no alternative but to put in the miles until I reached camp. By the time I got there, I was forced to set up in miserable conditions, even though the rain had stopped. The dampness was pervasive and it took forever simply to warm up and dry off, or even find something dry to wear. So far, we had been extremely lucky with the weather. Quite what people do with, say, ten straight days of rain, I couldn't possibly imagine. I was also hoping not to find out.

Front Royal—which marks the end of Shenandoah National Park—was only 26 miles ahead, and was going to be my next stop. To get there, I had to break the trip down into two 13-mile days, overnighting at Gravel Springs Hut. I was now back among the young guys I referred to earlier, enjoying their intermittent company.

The last wayside in Shenandoah wasn't a restaurant, it was more of a supply shop. A large group of us hung out for a couple of hours, grazing on jerky, tuna, burgers, fries, candy bars, and magnificent milkshakes, of which I had two. The shop was a general gathering spot for hikers and bikers, with the two communities coming together in a mutual bond of friendship, sharing their stories.

Once more full to the brim, I left the others behind in an attempt to make the shelter prior to the rain, and immediately ran into my seventh bear. The creature was balanced precariously up a tree. I don't mean to sound blasé, but I had been waiting for weeks to see my first bear and now I was getting them everywhere. It was always a joy to see these bears and my initial fears had entirely evaporated by the clear indication that they were even more frightened of me than I was of them. They are truly stupendous creatures, and I felt especially privileged to have had the opportunity to see them on their turf and not mine. Not everybody has the chance to put his life on hold for six months and go for a walk. The fact that I was able to do it, and see so many aspects of this wonderful country and its wild inhabitants, was an utter joy.

Another badly chosen camping spot gave me an unproductive night on the sleep front. I was ready for a night out of the woods. An easy 13-miler, along with my eighth bear, left me with conflicting feelings about Shenandoah.

It was mainly a green tunnel for most of the time, with the best views fashioned for tourists at the overlooks, yet the place gave me my bears. You've probably gathered from my gushing remarks that pretty much nothing could top that for me. You'd be right.

I also had a few thoughts about so-called yellow blazers: hikers who chose to shorten their journey by taking roads—lifts even—into towns, then resuming their hike from that town. This practice was particularly prevalent in Shenandoah, with regular and tempting access to roads and curious drivers, who would cheerfully engage a hiker and take them further down the road. Many of my peers were a little sniffy about the sanctity of the trail, and the need to be true to it by walking every single mile. I wasn't one of the sniffy ones, but I certainly wanted to walk every part of it. However, I learned to be more understanding of yellow blazers in this park.

We were all out for a great adventure and that adventure needed to be defined by our own standards. If that entailed missing a few miles here and there, then why not? Others, myself included, were able to spend more time in hostels and hotels, resting in relative comfort. Several hikers I met were unable to afford to ever get off the trail, other than to resupply and launder their clothes on occasion. Was their hike tougher than mine, even if they didn't hike the entire 2,185.3 miles? I would imagine that it was. I certainly wouldn't have liked to have stayed on the trail for six months with no respite. I learned in Shenandoah that we all have to come at the A.T. from different perspectives. Another hiker's method may not be our own, but it is equally valid.

There were life lessons to take from that realization, though those lessons really only fermented after I left the trail. For the time being, I was happy to accept my fellow hikers' stories for what they were, and to embrace each adventurer as sharing the same path as me, though each had their own idiosyncrasies. God knows, I certainly had my own as well.

Chapter 6: Front Royal to Harpers Ferry

My stay in Front Royal is a bit of a mystery to me, for I seem to have made no notes about what looks to be quite a pretty town. It made no impression upon me at all, which may have something to do with the fact that I stayed in yet another Super 8 motel, according to my receipts. While certainly adequate spots for sleeping, bathing, and laundering, these places rarely excite the spirit or leave a lasting mental image. As a consequence, all I can say is that I was there and that I left.

After Shenandoah, it was likely that there would be a bit of an anti climactic feel about the first day's hiking. However, it was another beautiful, warm day with a meadow first thing to soothe my soul. The meadow was particularly memorable for that rarest of things on the A.T.: a bench.

And it seemed that this wasn't just any old bench. I sat to enjoy my surroundings and took a brief panoramic video before deciding that a snack was in order. While I'd noted my loneliness around this time, I still thoroughly enjoyed my solitary snack breaks and, with a bench in the mix, this was one truly to be savored. I was unable to do it alone, though, for I was soon joined by a strange little man who pitched up with a tiny backpack. While I was ruminating over my Snickers, he hopped from one foot to the other like a five-year-old in need of the bathroom. He explained that the only hiking that he did was to this very spot, every day, in order to enjoy his lunch. I shifted up to the end of the bench and indicated that he should take the load off and join me. He seemed unwilling to do so, and continued his elaborate dance as I chomped away—companionably, I thought.

There is only so much conversation you can have with a hopping pixie, so I shouldered my pack and gave him the very American "Have a great day," and went on my way. I was no more than six feet from the bench when the hopping stopped and he was seated in his place, contentedly pulling out his lunch.

I guess it's a bitch when somebody comes along and interrupts your entire day, though I couldn't help but smile to myself at having got to his spot about two minutes before him. If that makes me a bad person, then so be it, but you need the odd victory against convention from time to time, and this was mine.

Another quiet, relatively gentle day got me to Dick's Dome Shelter by late afternoon and I was pleased to see a couple of interesting characters I'd met briefly before—Rudy and Daddy Long Legs.

Rudy was hiking the trail in memory of his grandmother, who had passed away after a long battle against Alzheimer's disease. Daddy Long Legs was documenting Rudy's emotional journey. They were ceremoniously burying small pieces of his grandmother's dress along the way, planning to inter the last piece at Katahdin. I hope I'm not doing a disservice to Rudy, but he exhibited an unusual intensity in both his story about his grandmother and his hiking. The intensity seemed fueled by his grief, motivating him to persevere in tough times on the trail. Daddy Long Legs was more laid back. He seemed to be documenting Rudy's story for a higher purpose, beyond just the hike itself.

I was struck once more by the willingness of hikers to open up about their own back story. I'm also aware that I've always been able to pry things from people that they may not have wished to tell me. Those who know me well will be nodding ruefully at this point.

For some reason, I had eaten and was in my tent just before 6 o'clock on this day. I was tired, though no more than usual, and I thought I'd take the opportunity for a quiet read. Schoolboy error. What seemed like two minutes later, I woke and glanced at my phone for the time. I'd been out for two hours and immediately thought, *I'll never get back to sleep now.* Another five minutes later, and it was 5:30 the following morning. I'd always been a fitful sleeper, and my tenting skills weren't generally helping with that. However, I must have found the perfect combination and had uninterrupted sleep through the night. Maybe it was because I knew what the day had in store for us all that I wanted to get an early start.

There was a choice to be made after nine or so miles at Rod Hollow Shelter. As a consequence, I resolved to get there as soon as possible for an early lunch and see how I felt. My sleep had certainly energized me, so I was already thinking about my alternatives. I could go for a tough 18-mile day that would involve taking on the frightening prospect of the "Roller Coaster." This was a series of intense, though fairly low hills along a ridge that came one after the other for an exhausting afternoon. A shortened version of that would be a 15-miler, ending at Sam Moore Shelter. The second choice would complete most of the "Roller Coaster." Of course, the third—and laziest—would be to spend the night at Rod Hollow and waste the afternoon.

As planned, I made Rod Hollow by about 11:30 a.m., and had already decided what I was going to do. I'd read in my guide that Bears Den Hostel had a "hiker's special" for $30, incorporating a bunk, laundry, a shower, breakfast the following morning, and, critically, a pizza and a pint of Ben & Jerry's ice cream. With such riches in store, what else could I choose? I was going for the 18-miler. I'd never had an end-of-the-day incentive to hike, and I can truly say that the Ben & Jerry's pushed me on more than I should admit. Indeed, I reached Sam Moore Shelter, still three miles shy of Bears Den, with thunder shaking through the forest and rain in the air, though not yet falling. At this point, I was all-in for the pint of Cherry Garcia, and I simply couldn't shake it from my mind. The fact that I covered those last three miles at about twice my normal pace is more indicative of my hiker hunger than my hiking legs. I got to Bears Den just before the rain started in earnest. I felt like a marathon winner as I checked in.

Poking one in the eye of the weather was a rare victory for me, but to be able to celebrate that victory with ice cream gave me a completely disproportionate feeling of elation that I'll remember forever.

In my bunk that night, I chuckled to myself about my reasons for the long hike that day. I also considered how close I was to a magical milestone. The hostel was situated just south of Snickers Gap, at mile 999, so I was about to pass the 1,000-mile marker the following morning. It was a big deal for me and I thought of my brother Mike.

We had spoken at mile 300, reflecting the distance we used to drive with our parents when we were kids, going on vacation to Wales. We'd also spoken after 600 miles, which of course related to our return journey. At 900 miles Mike had remarked on Facebook that his brother Steve had hiked the equivalent of driving from our old home in Southend to Wales, gone back home to check if he'd left the iron on, then driven back to Wales. He was proud of me and that felt good, lying in the dark as others snored around me.

A thousand miles! That was an achievement to be proud of, and I looked forward to the prospect of a picture the following day at the 1,000-mile marker. As it turned out, I was going to be spoiled for choice.

The mad dash for my Cherry Garcia had taken it out of me, so I modified my ambitions the following day and aimed for just an 11-miler. I would then be within about nine or ten miles of Harpers Ferry, traditionally regarded as the halfway point on the A.T. In actual fact, the true half distance was going to be another 70 miles along the trail, but Harpers Ferry retained the distinction as the A.T. grew ever longer.

Straight out of Bears Den Hostel I was looking for the 1,000-mile marker. I knew it would be upon me within the first hour. I was by myself, excited by this milestone, and hoped that it would be an inspirational point in my journey. Disappointingly, it was just a rock with moss scraped off to leave 1,000, followed by an exclamation point. I sat and took a selfie, sitting on the rock with an idiot grin on my face for posterity. I soon found out what the sign maker had done with the moss that had been removed. He or she had arranged it on the ground, about 100 yards further on, in the same configuration. Another sign, another idiot grin. I now felt sure that I truly had 1,000 miles under my belt, but was foiled again about 300 yards later.

There was a third, more permanent sign attached to a tree. Cue another pic. Later, I noticed that my grin faded with each new iteration of the marker. I was also aware that I'd done the miles, and that precisely where I'd passed the point wasn't terribly important.

This auspicious day was scheduled to end at the David Lesser Memorial Shelter. When I arrived there, Daddy Long Legs and Rudy were contemplating moving forward another three miles to Keys Gap. The big attraction was a store, just a quarter of a mile from the trail. The guys seemed quite relaxed for me to tag along, so we all headed out together, and I got into a close conversation with Rudy once more.

I felt part of a small team again, albeit for a short time. I was happy to be with them and they seemed comfortable with me. However, I knew we'd be splitting soon, because Daddy Long Legs wouldn't hike on a Sunday, and I had no such religious constraints. Because I had exceeded my mileage requirements by an additional three miles I was also putting more miles in the bank, building a substantial surplus to cope with the inevitable slowing down in the New England states.

Another burger was ferociously dispatched, along with several candy bars and sodas. We sat on the grass alongside the store, looking as if we hadn't eaten for weeks. We had made the decision to move on from the shelter, knowing that there was neither shelter nor campsite before Harpers Ferry. Consequently, we knew that we'd be roughing it for the night. Back at the entrance to the woods at Keys Gap, we found some decent flat spots. Unfortunately, they were less than ten yards from the road—and the roaring traffic. We didn't want to lose such potentially good spots and, weighing the pros and cons, we decided to set up there for the night.

We were full, so cooking was unnecessary, and we turned in at about 7:30. Despite the traffic, which seemed to speed up as it passed our spot, I had no trouble falling asleep, only waking once during the night. I was looking for something to read. I had my Kindle app on my iPod, as well as my iPhone, so I connected to the phone's hot spot, downloaded all five *Game of Thrones* books, and read for about half an hour. While I know that many hikers see the intrusion of technology as a negative, I couldn't help but feel wonder and gratitude for such an ability.

In a week of milestones, another one was attained the following morning when I crossed out of Virginia into West Virginia. Virginia had been my home for 550 miles, and had turned me from a complete novice to a halfway competent hiker. I hoped that the border would be celebrated in some fashion. I'm not sure if I simply missed it or if it just didn't exist, but I reached WVA32, and the state had clearly been exited without fanfare.

It was a time for quiet reflection, accompanied by a somnolent Snickers, as I took in the passing of this, the largest state on the trail. When I had entered Virginia, just before Damascus, I was still honing my skills, developing my hiker's legs, and even eating like a regular human being. I had now seen bears, countless snakes, been bitten by a dog, and spent a week or so at home. Additionally, I had developed a dangerous affinity to peanut butter and Snickers. The fabled "Virginia Blues" were much discussed, but I don't think I ever succumbed to them. I was a bit grumpy from time to time, but that happened in every state. Crossing a state line was the clearest indication of tangible progress in my quest to be a hiker, so, with only six miles of the A.T. in West Virginia, I was rapidly earning that designation. I enjoyed the thought immensely.

Harpers Ferry was an easy five-mile stroll that morning and was a place I'd been looking forward to for several days. The Appalachian Trail Conservancy was located there and was my first port of call. The A.T.C. was a neat place, with the staff taking our pictures for their album. I was number 856 of the year. Browsing through the book, I was able to track the progress of friends I had met on my journey. Many were now well ahead of me because of either my lack of pace or my time away from the trail. Looking at these pictures reinforced my loneliness, though it also strengthened my resolve to complete what I'd started.

But not before I'd had lunch.

I found Hannah's, a small, empty, barbecue-lunch spot that allowed me to ingest copious amounts of calories for my afternoon stretch. It was delicious. After lunch, the trail led me through the pretty tourist's stroll in the tiny historic part of town. I was on my way once more.

Chapter 7: Harpers Ferry to Pennsylvania

I headed away from Harpers Ferry, pausing to browse at several historic locations on my way, before crossing the Potomac. I set my sights on Ed Garvey Shelter, some six miles out of town, in Maryland, my sixth state.

There was a seemingly endless walk along the towpath next to the Potomac that was absolutely sweltering, with a slight incline for about three miles. Several hikers had taken the day off to spend time on the fast flowing river in boats and rubber rings. I saw my old friend, Billy Goat, who called out to me from one such boat as I crossed the bridge, just prior to the towpath. He must have recognized my slow, lumbering trudge. Sadly, I didn't run into Billy Goat again on the trail, though we texted from time to time, and he made Katahdin at the beginning of September.

The Ed Garvey Shelter was one of those shelters that left me in awe that people make so much effort on behalf of hikers. This was a real beauty, boasting a sleeping loft with plexiglass windows to catch the morning sun. There was a lot to be grateful for on this day. I was past Harpers Ferry, and, even though I wasn't halfway there in mileage, I was on the next leg of the journey.

When I'd had to curtail my hike because of that darned dog, one of my blog readers had noted that I needn't worry about the delay, as long as I was at Harpers Ferry by the July 4 holiday. If I could achieve that, I would then be able to finish at Katahdin before October 15—the cut-off date determined by Baxter State Park. It was still June, so I was ahead of the game. I'd also averaged just over 100 miles a week since my return, and was now hiking stronger than ever. That night, I slept well and looked forward to my second half.

Hiking the Appalachian Trail is an undertaking that requires many things. While you need strength, endurance, an ability to live in somewhat reduced circumstances, and mental toughness, you also need a fair amount of money. Of course, the money you need is dependent upon how often you go into town. Once there, you tend to hemorrhage the green stuff at an alarming rate. I had sold my business to do this and was no longer earning income, though I did draw a smallish pension. While my wife and I had told ourselves that selling the business would compensate for this lack of income, we both knew that we'd need to start earning again eventually.

I had been in the reinsurance industry for many years, and had accumulated something of a reputation, partly good, partly bad. I had often been called to provide expert witness testimony for, or against, certain insurance entities by lawyers, both in London and the U.S. When an insurance company was unable to come to settlement terms with its reinsurer, an arbitration system would be triggered. Each side would employ lawyers to put its case in arbitration proceedings. Those lawyers would contact experienced practitioners, and, for old hands like myself, this was a lucrative gig. In my time on the trail, I undertook four short assignments. These necessitated finding my way into a town with workable Wi-Fi, then reading large amounts of papers, writing an opinion, and emailing that opinion back to the lawyer who hired me. I would charge by the hour for my time, including reading, writing, and phone calls. In total, by doing this, I raised about $5,000.

Leaving Ed Garvey Shelter, I received a call from a lawyer in Chicago. The conversation went like this.

"Hullo."

He gave his name, telling me that he was calling about a case he had involving a certain issue. He hoped that I might be able to give him an opinion. I informed him that I was hiking, and that I was currently sitting on a log somewhere in Maryland. It's fairly tough to deter a lawyer, and he breezed on if this was a perfectly natural place for the two of us to be having this conversation. He was also, coincidentally, a hiker, so his client racked up a few extra bucks thanks to our hiking conversation.

"What's the case?" I asked, when it became apparent that he still wanted my opinion. He described his case.

"You'll lose," I said, and gave him my reasons.

"Could you put that in writing for me?" he continued, as if he hadn't heard.

"I'm hiking and about ten miles from the nearest road. If I get to the road, hitch a lift, and get to a hotel, I'll have to read your papers. Then, I'll have to write my report and your client will get the same answer I'm giving you now—for free. If I follow that course, your client will get a bill for about $2,000 and exactly the same answer."

"I need it in writing, to demonstrate due diligence," he responded.

And so it was that I followed that path, and found myself in a hotel, as opposed to a motel, in Hagerstown later that day. I know how ridiculous that all sounds, though it goes on the whole time. I won't go into the other occasions in which this happened, but they were similar, and netted me a good part of my expenses for the trip.

One distinct advantage of hiking in Maryland and, later, Pennsylvania, was that the trail would often take me through campgrounds or parks. These would usually give me access to water, always a critical element in walking the trail.

The hiking was very different, particularly in Maryland, where it was either flat, easy, and springy, or hilly, rocky, and downright dangerous. The latter hiking was damaging to my boots and feet, and certainly slowed me down. At the same time, I knew that Maryland was simply a precursor to Pennsylvania, and the rocks that I'd been assured were ahead. Having fallen down on a slippery rock for the twelfth time earlier that week, I had additional reason to be wary.

A few miles out of the shelter, just after I'd had my call with the lawyer, I passed through Gathland State Park, a wonderful area full of Civil War history. I was fortunate enough to run into a woman who seemed charmed by the British accent, and she allowed me to charge my rapidly depleting phone battery in her museum. I was drawn into the displays, and spent a fascinating hour learning about this area and the part it had played in the Civil War. My goal had originally been to get my phone charged, but my hostess seemed to feed off my interest, giving me such a deeply engaging experience that the hour seemed to vanish in an instant.

Brits tend to get a little dismissive about American history, given its lack of reach into the distant past. However, there is so much to see in and around the trail in this part of Maryland that I definitely came away with a new appreciation of the importance of that recent history, and the undeniable part it had in shaping the America of today. I was also aware that it was only by hiking the trail that I would ever have been privileged to have visited Gathland.

Diane had been eager to know where I was going to spend the night over the past few days and her insistence on knowing my whereabouts was starting to irritate me. I soon discovered why I was getting the Spanish Inquisition—or the Puerto Rican Inquisition, in her case.

Having hitched a lift from Turners Gap all the way into Hagerstown, I settled into my room, only to get a call from reception letting me know that I had a visitor. As I walked down the corridor, a couple of things fell into place in my head, and I silently apologized to Diane. An old friend, Ian Gilland, was visiting New York with his partner. He had been colluding with Diane as to where I was going to be on a given date, which happened to be this day. The conversation with Diane had started a while before, and he had expected me to be a lot further up the trail by now. Despite this setback, he had driven nearly 250 miles that day to visit me.

I was shocked as I realized it was him, and we hugged as he presented me with a British Olympic team hat. I was delighted. We immediately went out and devoured about 40 chicken wings, chocolate fudge cake, ice cream, and a couple of Buds. Gilbo, as I'd always known him, then returned me to my hotel, and headed back the 250 miles to New York. What a guy.

A gesture like that served to remind me just how much I must mean to some people, and I have always been extremely gratified to have made so many great friends over the years. Diane has now met quite a few of my old mates and discovered how special they are to me and I am to them. Every now and then, particularly now that I had so much time on my hands, it was incredibly satisfying to think about those I had touched in my life and those who had touched me. I found it more than a little life-affirming, since I clearly hadn't been a dick to everybody along the way. Gilbo may not have known it, but his visit meant so much more to me than I could express. He allayed my loneliness at almost the precise time that I needed it.

As always, the trail provides.

Quite apart from the fact that I'd earned $2,000 overnight for just giving my opinion—something I'm normally delighted to do without money changing hands—I was so buoyed by Gilbo's visit that the following morning I was back to the trail in a positive mood. I had quite a long cab ride back from Hagerstown. My driver was a charming older lady who jabbered away amiably for the entire journey. She asked me questions about the trail, then continually wandered off on a tangent when I answered.

It was a Sunday morning and, starting back at Turners Gap, I rejoined the trail. I was led immediately into a meadow, with a warm sun at my back, and a cool breeze in my face. Somewhat appropriately, given the day, I immediately passed a beautiful old church. I experienced a déjà vu moment from my childhood, for the whole setting bore such a strong resemblance to the English countryside.

Once I'd moved through this soporific scene, I found myself hiking at a comfortable, unhurried pace for a couple of miles. I then came to a side road that led to the first completed monument to George Washington. I'd studiously avoided side trails, preferring to use up my energy on the A.T. itself. However, I was in such a relaxed mood—and only had a relatively short day in front of me—that I wandered up to the monument to get another great view, and a slice of Americana.

At the top, I met up again with Naturally Hob, who always seemed to know about his surroundings. He filled me in on the monument. He was an unhurried observer of life, and I allowed myself to sit and listen to his commentary.

I had been using a solar charger, with varying success, to charge my phone on the trip. Unfortunately, the previous evening I had noticed that it was starting to come apart on one of the panels. This turned out to be the beginning of a catastrophic end, because it chose the site of the Washington Monument to completely disintegrate. I took several pictures of the damaged charger and emailed them to Diane, asking if she could get try to get a replacement from the manufacturer. Typically, she got onto it and one was on its way. I would absolutely hate to be a customer service representative at any company when my wife is on the other end of the phone. As if more were needed, this was another example of the importance of my little quarterback at home.

It was a delight to see a monument of historical significance in such a setting, overlooking a splendid valley in the early morning sun. I also knew I was dawdling, so I left somewhat reluctantly and picked up the pace.

Even on short days, the miles still needed to be hiked.

That night, at Ensign Cowall Shelter, after my easy, flat, 14-mile day, I ran into a couple of middle-aged lady hikers. Hobo Nobo and Caddyshack couldn't have seemed less suited as hiking partners, though they shared an unmistakable joy of the trail. Caddy was a mellow, quiet woman who had a smile for everybody, while Hobo was one of the great, loud characters on the trail. She was one of the standouts in my memory. I was always pleased to see them, and they seemed fairly pleased to see me. They may not have known it, but I always regarded them as prominent members of my peripheral "trail family" all the way to Katahdin.

Also at the shelter was a family of four, out on a short adventure and interested in thru-hikers as a breed, as well as the concept of a thru-hike itself. Over a cup of coffee the following morning, I sat with the dad, answering his many questions. He told me that his 16-year-old daughter was considering an attempt on the entire trail after high school. He said he had been impressed and reassured by hikers he had met, and his fears for her safety had been considerably eased. I can't overstate how much it buoyed me hearing how inspiring such an adventure is. The conversation reminded me how lucky I was that circumstances had conspired to permit me the chance to do this. We all need those reminders from time to time.

Leaving camp the following morning, I upped my game once more, with an 18-mile hike planned. I was heading for Pen-Mar Park by lunchtime with a mission in mind. I'd heard that pizza could be ordered for delivery to the park and, never one to pass up the opportunity of a large meat pizza, I set out on that mission.

At the park, I ran into Lumberjack—still wearing his lilac lacrosse shirt—and Nobody, an earnest young German guy, who often ran along the trail for no apparent reason other than he was having such a great time. The three of us ordered pizza and sat charging our phones at an available power point as we waited for the delivery.

Exiting the park, we crossed the Mason Dixon Line, separating the South from the North. We had passed another significant milestone, for we were entering Pennsylvania, probably the least-loved state on our itinerary. The fact that it was also one of the longest—at about 230 miles—gave us all pause. We knew that things were about to get tougher, and we weren't disabused of this assessment in any significant manner during the next 230 miles.

Chapter 8: Welcome to Pennsylvania

Hiking with a belly full of pizza was always comforting and this day was no exception. The early miles of Pennsylvania were largely similar to Maryland, so I made decent progress, reaching Tumbling Run Shelter soon after 6 o'clock. It was great to meet up with Tomahawk and Doc again, along with Lumberjack and Nobody, while a young married couple, Turbo and Poho, had also joined the group. I never had a problem interacting with the younger hikers on the trail, and I was always grateful that they were happy enough hanging around with the old guy. I'm guessing that I was a bit of an oddity to them and thus tolerable.

Tumbling Run was an interesting shelter because there were two small shelters, about 20 yards apart, linked by a pergola-type structure and two picnic tables. There were a lot of people camping in the woods nearby, including Hobo Nobo and Caddy, so we had our own small village once more. I heard over breakfast the following morning that one of the shelters had been considerably noisier than the other overnight. A couple of champion snorers seemed to have taken up residence side by side, though none of the hikers would either admit, or accuse, the culprits. I couldn't have cared less, of course, for I had found a decent spot to tent about 50 yards away.

I set up camp about 15 yards from another older guy, probably in his early- to mid-50s. He was with his dog, Lucy, and, having briefly taken in that this man and dog were camping next to me, I noticed that he only had a right arm and a right eye. We struck up something of a desultory conversation, avoiding the obvious dearth of limb and eye, while chatting about everything else. Eventually, I asked him his name and he came up with the delightfully self-deprecating name of Lefty. I looked at him for an instant, before we both burst out laughing. Quite what I would have done if he'd said Cyclops, I really couldn't tell.

The ice broken, he went on to tell me how he had lost both his arm and his eye, though he had clearly come to terms with his situation. We both cracked up from time to time as he described one disaster after another. Life had been hard on Lefty. He saw the woods as his safe place, where he felt the most comfortable.

While he was talking, he was doing what we all do at camp, including putting up his tent and filtering water. As had often happened before on this trip, I was struck at how some people were able to meet and overcome hardships. Lefty will stay in my memory, for he refused any help to put up his tent or hold his water bottle steady. He just got on with it, improvising his way through, and ending up with both a sturdy-looking tent and plenty of clean water.

Beyond this determination, he was also sad. He remarked that he would never find a woman, and that Lucy was really the only company he had. In my tent later, Lefty's sadness played in my head, and I saw how tough his challenges must be every day. Even sadder was the fact that he was forced to face them alone. He remained an unhappy thought for several weeks after I met him. I hope he is well.

Caledonia State Park was my intended lunch spot the next day, with the promise of a burger uppermost in my mind. The park had its own public pool, so there was also the possibility of a swim.

The day started warm and sunny and, with a ten-mile stint before lunchtime, I got out of camp fairly briskly. The ten miles were polished off in only four hours—the hike being fairly benign—though an early climb up Chimney Rocks exercised my sweat glands once more. At the park, the trail emerged into a clearing, with picnic tables all around, and I joined my younger, fitter friends. We based ourselves around those tables, under the shade of huge trees, and away from the public. It was as if we self-censored ourselves. We drifted in twos and threes to the concession stand, where calorific goodies were to be had. I ordered the mandatory burger, and asked the guy in the shop if I could charge my phone behind the counter. He took it from me, so I was grounded for a while. I went to lie on the grass, under a tree and away from everybody else.

I had jumped into rivers and ponds on the trail, but I felt dreadfully self-conscious about stripping down to my shorts and plunging into a public pool. Incidentally, the others felt much the same. Families were gathered together, and it didn't seem right to interject ourselves into this morass of people who were clearly living differently from us. I fully recognize that this was my problem, not theirs, but I couldn't help but feel the difference. So I lay there, sweltering in the grass, while the means to cool down glittered in the sunlight only 50 yards away.

With my phone and my stomach fully charged, I set out on my second ten-mile section of the day, across flat terrain, towards Birch Run Shelter.

I'd been making great progress, keeping up the pace from the morning, when, after an hour or two, I heard the ominous sound of thunder in the distance. The noise alone wouldn't have normally concerned me too much, because it reverberated from a long way away. However, when the second clap came, I knew it was heading towards me.

The threat remained for the next couple of hours, and I started to think that I might get away with it, since the storm appeared to have given me rather a wide berth. Suddenly, and with no clue that it was about to find me, I was hit by the full fury of the storm. The rain was torrential, utterly soaking me within seconds, while the lightning lit up the forest all about me. I trudged forward through the rapidly liquefying path, and arrived at the shelter completely drenched. I had to strip straightaway into my only remaining dry clothes—a pair of swimming trunks and my camp shirt. My temperature had plunged, and I badly needed to get out of every stitch of clothing I had on, just to warm up. It was a small shelter, with insufficient room for the ten-strong group of us.

I managed to hang all my clothes in a forlorn attempt to dry them, should drying conditions arise, but it was hopeless. I needed the rain to subside, because there was no room in the shelter for me. I started to contemplate a night on the picnic table as a last resort. After an hour, the rain slowed, then ceased entirely, and five or six of us hurriedly took advantage of the lull to set up our tents, and retire for the night. There had been a number of new faces at the shelter, and some of them were now alongside me in the woods. One of these was a very funny Irishman, uninspiringly named Ireland, who kept everybody's spirits up. I ended a tricky day by laughing, which is never a bad way to drop off to sleep.

Just four miles into the following morning, and 74 miles after I'd passed Harpers Ferry—the traditional halfway point—I passed the true halfway point. It was at mile 1,092.6, and was adorned with an elaborate structure to commemorate the event. Sadly, for my picture, I had dressed that morning in the driest clothes I could find. This meant that I was wearing the sweaty ones of two days before, along with my natty swimming shorts. For such a major milestone, this wasn't a good look. To be frank, it wasn't a good look under any circumstances.

Knowing how long it had taken to get to this point, I stepped across the imaginary line. I was nearer to Katahdin than to Springer for the first time. I had an overwhelming feeling that I had to do the mileage again, and I harbored my usual doubts about my ability to do so. Would my feet hold up? Would I fall badly? What about my ankles? Did I have the strength? I was mildly impressed with myself that I didn't include the prospect of ending up mauled by a bear. These doubts would flicker through my mind at various times in my journey, though I had always been able to talk myself out of them. On this occasion, I turned my attention to my upcoming halfway celebration at the Half Gallon Challenge in Pine Grove Furnace State Park—just five miles ahead. As a celebration it sucked, though I wasn't going to discover that until early the following morning. Very early.

The Half Gallon Challenge is a silly rite of passage that some hikers put themselves through. The more sensible ones choose to duck out of the challenge, contenting themselves by watching their fellow hikers behave irrationally. I didn't even contemplate rational behavior.

I arrived at the scene of the crime—the General Store—before noon, laying out my soaked clothes across the various picnic tables. I thought I'd wait for them to dry out in the sun as

I took on the Challenge. This was excellent marketing by the General Store, as hikers chose from a liberally stocked freezer containing only ice cream. We were then charged for the privilege of shoveling ungodly amounts of the gloopy stuff down our throats. The lilac-clad Lumberjack had already had his fill, taking about 50 minutes to get through it. He looked a bit green around the gills as he sat on the porch watching the spectacle.

I chose vanilla and mint chocolate chip in an attempt to shake it up a bit, starting with the larger tub of vanilla. Working my way through it without drama in about ten minutes, the vanilla went down easily. With just the smaller mint chocolate chip to go, I got a little cocky. I called out Lumberjack and a few others as pussies, yet the moment I opened that second tub, the wheels fell off. Suddenly, my vanilla confidence had evaporated into a minty mess, and I struggled through the smaller tub, eventually finishing in 27 minutes. My reward was a slightly disappointing wooden spoon from the shop. It was the type you get when you open an ice cream tub, with some sort of notation to the effect of your recent success in the Challenge. Despite my cynicism regarding this prize, I confess that I still own my hard-won trophy.

With a pack of dry clothes and a stomach full of gurgling ice cream, I decided to head on alone. I was hoping to make the next shelter, Tagg Run, less than eight miles away, with the weather closing in. My luck held, and I made it in plenty of time for dinner. Already at the shelter was a young guy I'd camped next to a few weeks before, Bilbo, as well as a group of four hikers—Big Sexy, J-Rex, and the Maine Sisters, otherwise known as Toots and Navigator.

Bilbo kept himself to himself and retired early. Big Sexy was a friendly, red-headed, smiling lad who, when I asked him why he was so named, just shrugged and laughed. I saw neither of these guys after that night, while the three girls were part of my hike for much of the next 600 miles. I grew to appreciate them more as time went on.

I chose pasta for dinner that night. I had totally forgotten that the combination of pasta and ice cream, in my past, had often produced fairly dire consequences. I didn't even consider it while boiling my pot.

In the early hours of the following morning, in my tent, I realized for the first time that I may have made an error by eating so much pasta on top of my ridiculous amount of ice cream. The feeling was exacerbated when I turned on my side, and my stomach let out an audible, and painful, groan. *Hmmm*, I thought, more out of curiosity than anything else. This quickly turned to *Oh, my God,* as the inevitable conclusion became apparent. Suddenly, I was scrambling to leave my tent, because everything wanted to exit my body as soon as possible from every available orifice. Outside, it was pitch dark, I was barefoot, virtually naked, and desperate. Nature isn't to be ignored, so two dramatic evacuations took place: the first, by me, from my tent, and the second, by everything else, from my body. While I am aware of the importance to hikers of the concept of "Leave No Trace," I confess to an epic fail on this particular occasion. I suppose I can only plead mitigating circumstances.

Restored once more to my tent and to the warmth of my quilt, I breathed again and mistakenly relaxed for a moment. The warning that I had 20 minutes later was both more sudden and more urgent. I had barely poked my head out of my tent while retching, and only managed to hold everything in before eventually diving into the bushes for an even more intense purging. It was dreadful. I spent the remainder of the night on alert for another episode but, thankfully, I was done, and daylight came without further incident.

There really is no fool like an old fool, is there?

I was physically and, quite literally, drained, and felt completely incapable of hiking anywhere.

From my guidebook I recalled that I'd be crossing a road within half a mile, and that there was a relatively nearby inn, at Mount Holly Springs, that provided shuttles for hikers. A quick phone call established a rendezvous point, and I staggered the half-mile to the road, before sitting in a heap and waiting for my shuttle.

As I sat there, exhausted by the night, I had another internal battle over how stupid I'd been. Several of the youngsters had passed on the ice cream, but I, believing myself to be insulated from the laws of gastrointestinal science, had acted like a preening fool. I had tried to prove myself capable of keeping up with my peers, though had failed miserably when I ladled pasta on top of lactose. Not for the first time in my life—nor even the first time on this hike—I berated myself for this need to do or try things that were clearly not good for me. I'd had a few low points and this was another.

Consequently, less than an hour into my day, I pitched up at Holly Inn and Restaurant in a pitiful state. I was completely unable to eat or drink, despite being severely dehydrated. I was miserable to my core.

Then my luck turned.

As so often happened on this magical trail, aid came to me. This time, the aid came in the form of the wonderful Fran and Steve Davis, friends who had been following my blog, and who happened to live in Pennsylvania. I had only met Fran once and had never met Steve. They were the parents of a young woman—Alicia—who is one of my wife's dearest friends. Apparently, they had been reading my blog and had bought into the magic of the A.T., even providing Trail Magic on occasion, where the trail came close to their home.

They had intended to see me a little further up the trail, and, when Fran called, I told her of my predicament. They drove for more than an hour to not only help me with my laundry but also to drive me around and try to find gas for my stove. They brought a bunch of supplies with them and were, frankly, just the tonic that I needed at that time. I'd had Trail Magic through my hike, but this brand of Trail Magic was so personal and so heartfelt that it touched me and sustained me for a very long time. When Fran and Steve left, I still felt far too weak to hike, so I decided to stay another night to allow myself the chance to replenish my body. Fran and Steve had replenished my soul.

To this point, I had reached the stage that sleeping in my tent allowed me a better night's sleep than sleeping in a hotel or motel bed. However, that night I slept for a solid nine hours. I woke feeling so much better that it was startling, though I stuck with my intention of the previous night. I took the opportunity to relax and update my blog, spending the afternoon in the bar at the Inn. I watched a couple of World Cup matches, and resumed my assault on yet another menu.

I'd learned another lesson, which you may think that I should have learned by the age of seven. Ice cream and pasta, in combination, would never be part of my diet again. I'm pleased to report that I've stuck with this one.

The day had also shown me that, in your darkest times, there is always a way forward, albeit one which may not be immediately apparent. There would be more dark days, yet I always knew I could overcome them. That realization became another breakthrough in my growing skills as a hiker.

Chapter 9: Hitting the rocks

The two-day hiatus caused by my own stupidity came to an abrupt end the following morning. I had spent a restless night prior to hitting the trail once more, and was rather nervous that I'd be able to get back into the swing of things with sufficient impetus to maintain my mileage. I was entertaining doubts that I would have previously just glossed over, but these fears were real and starting to undermine me. Never one to outwardly lack confidence, I was finding this new aspect of my character to be both surprising and unwelcome. I now see that this is just part of the process that all hikers have to go through at some time during their hike.

The kind lady operating the shuttle for the hotel drove me back to my previous finish point. I delayed my start, falling into a conversation with a couple of day hikers who were about to hike in the opposite direction. By the time I got underway, I felt a little shaky, with the remnants of the ice cream still perhaps having their effect, though I'm sure that my earlier doubts were resurfacing. Once I got back into my stride, though, I felt strong enough to make a confessional video about my shortcomings and felt better for having got things off my chest.

With my hiking back in equilibrium, I was now able to settle down and enjoy the day. I had a very modest target—Boiling Springs—which made for a short, 11-mile day. Fran and Steve were visiting me once more, having insisted upon driving down to meet me with a gas canister for my stove, just in case I wasn't able to get one in Boiling Springs. Finding gas canisters was becoming a bit of an issue at this stage, so I was grateful for their generosity, particularly when I couldn't find one in this otherwise charming town.

The trail was now running along a low part of Pennsylvania, rarely reaching above 1,000 feet. This particular day took me through more meadows and fields, with less forest than usual. That was because the trail was going close to highly populated areas around this part of the state, and the A.T.C. wanted to keep the whole thing as rural as possible. To my mind, it came up with a great compromise: namely, routing us through fields and the edges of forests to avoid using roads. I loved it.

I arrived about five minutes before I had arranged to meet up with Fran and Steve, and was greeted with a wonderfully bucolic view as I walked alongside the lake that dominates the town. The whole place seemed very reminiscent of England in the middle of the last century, with local shops and a tavern at the heart of the community. The warmth of the sun added to the sleepy atmosphere.

Fran and Steve had been there a while, so we headed straight to the tavern for some air conditioning, a burger, and a beer. After lunch, we wandered across the road to a local outfitter, though this business turned out to be more directed to the fishing community, and had no gas canisters. However, the owner was a fascinating guy—a real outdoorsman—and we hung out chatting with him for nearly an hour. When we left, Fran and Steve headed home, having handed over my precious gas, while I returned to the tavern. There, I met a couple of other hikers, Rambler and Dos Lekis. We had a few beers and watched another World Cup game while I recharged my phone.

The only place to tent in this delightful place was a free campsite to the south of the town. I retraced my steps and found myself back in the fields once more, eventually coming upon the designated area. Four guys had set up and were fragrantly relaxing, if you get my drift. They invited me to join them but I wanted to set up my tent. I also came to the conclusion that, while the ice cream was one thing, compounding the error with a new venture into enhanced smoking might be pushing the envelope a touch too far. The guys warned me that the trains run all night and "can be quite loud." This turned out to be an understatement of massive proportions.

I was just dozing off when I heard a rumble that seemed like it could be thunder. However, it turned immediately, and frighteningly, into a rushing, roaring sound that passed so close that I actually ducked, lest it come directly through my tent. It was, at best, startling, and was repeated several times through the night. Indeed, at 5 a.m. I thought I heard the rails rattle as a heavily laden cargo train hammered its way past my tent, though the rattling may very well have been my teeth.

Despite this truncated night, I managed to get some sleep. I got onto the road fairly early in the hope that Boiling Springs would be able to provide me with a breakfast worthy of its status as my new favorite town on the trail. Ten minutes later, I was sitting in front of two fried eggs, bacon, home fries, plus an overflow plate of French toast and syrup. Add a coffee to the mix, as well as *The New York Times* on my iPad, and I felt very comfortable for the next hour or so.

Realizing that the miles were not going to walk themselves, I grudgingly left the town, and quickly downgraded my estimate for the day to Darlington Shelter, just 14 miles away. I'd originally hoped to reach the next shelter, giving me a short trot into Duncannon the following morning. Unfortunately, my Starbucks moment back in Boiling Springs had thrown all the timing off, so 14 miles it was.

Sometimes, you just have to sit back and smell the coffee.

My guidebook had suggested more of the same that day and I was certainly up for a bit of meadow walking to help digest my breakfast. The profile looked completely flat for most of the way, only climbing up 750 feet just before the shelter. There wasn't quite as much meadow walking as I'd imagined, though sufficient for any hiker to appreciate the efforts that the Appalachian Trail clubs make on behalf of hikers to keep them away from roads.

I was often walking right on the edge of forests, just in the woods. At these sections I heard great sounds, with the cacophony of birds interspersed with the low sounds of trains warning the populace of some distant town. I seemed to have heard trains a lot over the previous couple of hundred miles, though not, fortunately, as close as those the previous night. A deer ran out right in front of me and bounded away. With everything so close to a more urban setting, these encounters with wild animals enhanced my appreciation of the wilderness. I should also add that this particular deer made me jump out of my skin, but the sentiment remains, as the presence of animals, in their own environment, never got old for me.

Duncannon was apparently one of those must-see locations for hikers, though I never understood quite why that should be. I had originally intended to take a zero day there, but my ice cream adventure had put paid to that. It was only a 12-mile hike from Darlington Shelter, so I modified my target for the day. The new plan was to get into town, and pick up two packages—food from Diane and the replacement solar charger. I was going to have a burger and a couple of beers at The Doyle—the famous hikers pub—and then head straight out to Clark's Ferry Shelter, only four or five miles outside town.

This turned the day into a 15- or 16-mile hike, starting on a sticky Monday morning. I was moving along well, anticipating my burger and beer, when, talking on the phone to Diane, I completely missed a turning. I headed on down the mountain, only to find myself in a community with not a white blaze to be seen.

It is a remarkable aspect of the A.T. that the white blaze is so critical to all hikers' well-being that there was an anxious yearning to see one when one hadn't been spotted for a few minutes. So it was on the outskirts of Duncannon that morning. I reached this small urban community, some half a mile after my phone call, with nothing to take me further on my journey.

I could easily have turned to my iPhone, located The Doyle via GPS, then found the best walking route. To me, the E.F.I. hiker, that was simply not on the cards. In such circumstances, the only thing to do was to turn around and retrace my steps, however uncomfortable that was going to be. I had to scramble back up the mountain, and continue, effectively backwards, until I found a blaze. Eventually, I was able to get to where I'd been half an hour previously. Still, I was back on track and had done the right thing, though these silly diversions always ticked me off.

The trail into Duncannon had been slightly rerouted to avoid a missing bridge, but I soon found The Doyle, along with what eventually became a dozen or so hungry and thirsty hikers during that lunchtime.

It was a run-down old place, bearing all the hallmarks, but none of the charm, of a previous era. The beer and burger both hit the spot and the staff was great, but I wondered what all the fuss about Duncannon had been based upon. Several hikers later told me that the bedrooms at The Doyle were awful, as well as a probable fire hazard, so this was a zero day I was glad to miss.

I left to retrieve my packages from the post office, consolidated my pack, and started the long, very hot trek out of town. The walk included a lengthy, very boring High Street, two bridges, and a climb to escape the horrendous noise of cars. Maybe it was because I never find myself alongside crowded roads in my normal life, but the cars were overpoweringly noisy. I was actually shocked at how alien everything seemed to be. Once I started climbing, though, the noise subsided and normal calm was resumed.

I'd crossed the Susquehanna River and, turning to look back at the river and the town, I was struck at how much better both looked from a height, in the quiet, than they did from the ground. I was back in the woods and, as far as I'm concerned, you can keep Duncannon and The Doyle.

Until now, around 80 miles into Pennsylvania, the rocks had been challenging from time to time, though not overwhelmingly so. I'd even started to wonder if the hype about

Rocksylvania had been totally overblown. The climb up from the Susquehanna River made me revise my view.

As the climb started, there was an initial lull that, though fairly steep, wasn't too difficult. I was being carried away from the noise below, for which I was grateful, so I didn't really pay attention to the growing number of rocks to negotiate. They proliferated from then on. The hike to Clark's Ferry Shelter turned out to be my baptism into the fact that the hype wasn't in the least bit overblown.

I thought I'd make the three miles in about an hour and a half, but it was fully two-and-a-half hours, maybe even three, before I turned up. I was exhausted. The last mile into the shelter had been a nightmare, hiking as if part of an intricate jigsaw that put a premium on foot and pole placement to avoid a nasty fall. I was stunned to experience the escalated difficulty, and all my doubts returned in their time-honored fashion. I knew that I had 140 miles to go before I got to the New Jersey border, so I fervently hoped that they wouldn't all be like that last mile.

The shelter itself had no nearby tenting sites, so a bunch of us formed our own tiny village a few hundred yards from the shelter. Most importantly, we were close enough to the water source. We had all been unnerved by the difficulties of the day. We'd also been warned that the stretch we'd entered was going to be challenging in terms of water availability. I made a point of taking in as much water from this source as possible, glugging down a couple of liters to start my day the next morning. I then filled my bottle and water bladder with another two liters.

It was nowhere near enough.

I think I started out in the wrong frame of mind that day. I knew water would be an issue, although I underestimated quite how much. It was one of my worst days on the trail to this point, even though I achieved my distance of 13.3 miles. There was intense heat, it was rocky, and I had totally unprepared myself for the prospect of 12 miles with no readily available water source.

The rocks sapped both my energy and my spirit. I felt down for pretty much the whole day. I'm aware that a large part of the world lives without water security, but I had simply chosen to take an insufficient amount. Quite how terrifying the reality of not having the option to drink good water can be, I just couldn't imagine. When I eventually reached a good source, I greedily gulped down two liters immediately. For me, the day was as good as over.

I was at Clarks Valley, on PA325, and the positioning of shelters hadn't been working in my favor. I had visited Peters Mountain Shelter after about seven miles that morning. The water source was down a dramatically steep, blue-blazed trail of almost 300 rock steps, directly in front of the shelter on the north side of the mountain. Those steps didn't present a realistic option to me. I sat there, with nobody else around, weighing other options I might have. I still had over a liter of water in my Nalgene, and considered that precipitous walk down to the source. My tiredness overcame what I knew to be the right conclusion, which would have been to make that trek down to fresh water. I convinced myself that the path to Clarks Valley, and the next water, wasn't too taxing in elevation terms, so I chose to move on. By the time I reached the road, and the stream beside it, I was done. I crossed the road with my precious water, setting up my tent about 20 feet off the trail, quite close to a river.

There were a couple of other hikers a bit deeper in the woods, though I only had a few words with them as a storm was approaching within the next hour. I wanted to finish the day as quickly as possible inside my tent. Once set up, I slept for over an hour, then woke to hear the approaching thunder. The hour's sleep had revitalized me somewhat, and I was snug inside my tent, though it was still light outside. I heard a great whooshing sound as, first, the high wind then, second, the rain, descended upon my tent, hitting it suddenly like a sucker punch. It was more than a touch alarming and I became concerned that the tent might not hold up to such ferocity. Fortunately, it only lasted as violently as that for about thirty minutes. I was constantly watching for any incursion of water, or even dislodged tent stakes, so I was relieved when everything settled down. Having my tent collapse around me would have been a new low. The storm calmed, then left me to my thoughts and, eventually, to my sleep.

I registered an early morning record after my damp night, getting on my way by 6:35 a.m. Unfortunately, to achieve this record, I skipped breakfast. Ignoring my oatmeal would normally be a prelude to listlessness on my part, and, once more, it turned out to be so.

I started to feel a little like I had the day before, so I flopped my pack on the ground after about a mile, pulled out my stove, and breakfasted right in the middle of the trail. I felt like a hobo on a street corner. Satisfied, I felt refreshed and, with plenty of water, I hiked immeasurably better than the day before. I even had time to visit the immaculate Rausch Gap Shelter for a leisurely lunch of mashed potatoes and tuna.

This shelter, built in 1972—though lovingly maintained—had a couple of features that made it worth a visit, even though it was about a third of a mile off the trail. Indeed, had I not already set my sights on Swatara Gap, I'd have stayed there for the rest of the day. Apart from the fact that the place looked as if it had a regular sweeping, there was a rather natty circular table built onto a handy tree right in front of the shelter. The shelter also boasted one of the best and most convenient water sources, with a spring-fed pipe. Only yards away, it was built into the neatly maintained landscaping, running devastatingly cold water from underneath the nearby rocks. If I ever did this hike again—and I won't—I would certainly plan a few days ahead to spend the night at this shelter.

I had a leisurely six miles to go to get to Swatara Gap and enjoyed the stroll. However, I was liberally berating myself for my lack of care the day before, so that kept me entertained.

I eventually emerged at Swatara Gap, and called Diane to work out both a room at the Days Inn and a cab to come and fetch me. To complicate what would normally seem to be an easy process, my phone was running low on juice, which meant that I was unable to spend much time either talking with her or finding a cab. As always, she came through while I sat beside the road, with my phone charger grabbing as much sun as possible to generate sufficient charge to get a few more percentage points on my phone. Sometimes, taking it from three percent to six percent made all the difference.

Luckily, this lack of phone time allowed me to avoid hearing about a ridiculous conversation that she must have had with my driver. He lived several miles away from my intended destination, and wanted me to walk towards him. He refused to drive further than an underpass that was about two miles from Swatara Gap. Quite why this oaf was so unrelenting I never got to understand, even though he was perfectly chatty with me once I got to his car, as if he'd fulfilled his driving obligations. He did point out that lifts to and from the trail weren't financially efficient for him, and that there were no other cab drivers near this rural place. Our conversation came to an end at the Days Inn, where I encountered another expression of disdain towards hikers. Apparently, the hiker rate gets you the basement room, in which there is no window and a dank darkness that is somehow more threatening than the middle of the forest.

This was a strange place, with takeout pizza the local highlight, so I availed myself of that, watched a bit of TV, and wrote the day off.

Chapter 10: More rocks and more people

It was around these middle miles that I felt the need for something more than my apology tour and the quiet around me. I had been trying to come to terms with my life decisions, and that may well have started to get me down somewhat. I'd also noticed that I was recording my loneliness far more than I remember feeling at the time. In retrospect, my increasing solitude seemed to coincide with my use of podcasts and music through my phone.

Dwindling human interaction was an obvious development, given the numbers dropping out. Many of my peers were partial to solitude, but it weighed heavily on me. The podcasts, then the audiobooks, and the music helped me by providing a voice in my ear. However, those voices seemed to disconnect me from the trail in subtle ways that didn't register with me while I was listening to them. In general, I was happier when the headphones were in my pockets and not in my ears. But they remained firmly in place during certain parts of the day, for the rest of my journey. Listening to something other than the quiet of the woods became a crutch I couldn't completely throw away.

Leaving the following morning promised to be as problematic as getting there. I called the cab company and had the pleasure of talking to one of the most deliberately stupid people I've interacted with in my life. I realized that I was unlikely to find somebody enthusiastic about driving me back to the trail, but this charm school reject was clearly in the business of pissing off customers to the best of his ability. To be fair, he was very good at it.

I called at 7:30 a.m., telling him that I needed a cab for 9 o'clock. He was having none of it, telling me that I should call when I was ready to leave.

"I'll be ready at 9 o'clock," I replied.

"Well, call me then," was his response.

I couldn't be bothered to get all British on him and hung up the phone, fuming, and resigned myself to hitching the three- or four-mile return journey.

As predicted, I was ready to leave at 9 o'clock, having gathered a few necessities at the Hess gas station across the road.

I positioned myself just past the turn out from the gas station, plastering on my hopeful smile while I stuck out my thumb. As luck would have it, the second truck to pass my way contained a human being with a love for hiking. He stopped, told me to lob my stuff in the back and we chatted about the A.T. for a very pleasant five or ten minutes. He then deposited me in exactly the right spot. Sometimes it's your day and sometimes it isn't.

It is normally the small things that can make or break your day. Looking back at videos of the trail, I have been touched at just how much impact tiny acts of kindness had on me. Early morning positivity always resulted in a better hike.

Diving into the woods once again, I knew that I had a bit of a hike up for a few miles, but then I'd be on a ridge for the rest of the day. As I started the climb, I was caught by Bassman, a decent guy and a section hiker I'd met a few days before. He was a little younger than me, probably in his early 50s, so we were able to move along at roughly the same pace. We fell into step with one another, Bassman leading the way up a steep climb.

We spent a great day together, chatting easily back and forth, then taking lunch and getting water after about seven miles. His section hike was going to be over at PA501, at Pine Grove, which was also my target for the day. The 501 Shelter was set back a hundred or so feet from the same road. We said our farewells and I followed the path to the shelter. It was a four-walled building, with about a dozen bunks, so I slung my pack on a top bunk as I renewed old acquaintances and made a few new ones.

I'd told Bassman where I was heading and, about ten minutes after I'd settled in, he turned up at the shelter with some Trail Magic of his own, bringing Gatorade and other goodies. What a star. Bassman had been the perfect antidote to my loneliness and we got on so well that we even spoke during the day about the possibility of hiking again together in Maine, in September. These things are often said but rarely come to fruition, although I felt strongly that I'd see him again.

I did, but not for many more miles.

The shelter was sufficiently close to the road to allow us to order pizza, so pies were duly ordered and delivered. With such a large bunch of people in the shelter there was another lively evening and, with that and my day with Bassman, my mood had lightened considerably.

We spoke that evening about Lyme disease, which was an ever-present danger on the trail. One of the younger guys, Chip, was not only being treated for Lyme, but, along with two other younger men, was also being treated for rabies. This was more as a precaution than a response to a diagnosed disease. One of the lads had been bitten by a skunk, while the other two were bitten by a sick bat, at Penn Mar Park. Chip, one of the bat-bitten boys, woke to find that the critter was tangled in his hair and had crapped on his face. Treatment for rabies seemed eminently reasonable to me.

The Maine Sisters, along with J-Rex, were also in the bunkhouse. They had decided that simply ordering pizza wasn't for them; they were going to the shops to stock up. When they returned, they emptied out their haul with an almost messianic exultation, laughing out loud as each individual item appeared. They had clearly over-indulged themselves but couldn't care less, proceeding to eat relentlessly to cut down the weight in their packs. I always enjoyed the company of these three girls. They were constantly laughing and reveling in both the trail and each other. I'm sure they had tough moments, but I never heard a harsh word from any of them, and I always appreciated their positivity.

I had a bit of a date with destiny the following day, though I had no inkling of it when I started out.

I was pushing for a 15-mile day, quite a target in Pennsylvania given the terrain. In this state, it is all about the rocks, not the climbing. The guide indicated a level path, but you'd never know it once you hit those rocks. I managed to get myself motivated and out by 6:45 a.m. The rocks were tricky and tiring in equal measure and, by PA183, I was more than ready for a spot of lunch.

I ran into three guys at the road. Survivor had been joined by his twin brother on the trail for a few days, and they were taking a breather at the road. With them was the enigmatically named James, who apparently wrote his name in all capital letters. James—or JAMES—was getting a shuttle to town for a post office drop. Eventually, they all left me to my tuna wrap. Seconds after James had driven off, a guy pulled into the parking area and asked me if I wanted a cold beer with my lunch. Trail Magic, with me the only recipient. I was normally the one just missing out, so I felt justifiably smug at my good fortune and downed a beer gratefully.

I should have paid more attention to the potential ramifications of the sign at the entry to the blue-blazed path that led to Eagles Nest Shelter: "Bad News: The privy is closed. Good News: There's a shovel. Bad News: Rock beats shovel."

This was a less-than-subtle warning that hikers would be crapping *au natural* the following morning. I chuckled at the sign, having passed that hurdle many miles back, and often in the interim. As I walked down the blue-blazed trail into the shelter, I tried to imagine just how bad a privy must have been to close it. I shuddered at the thought. The Maine Sisters and J-Rex were there, along with Survivor and his brother, as well as Voodoo, another young, fearless woman, and Yeti Legs.

This was my first time meeting Yeti Legs and I confess to something of a *what the fuck* moment. He was an extremely affable, entirely unselfconscious guy aged only 19. He was smart, engaging, and very funny. What most people will remember about Yeti Legs, I would imagine, would be his penchant for wearing just a pair of gray underpants and nothing else. His ever-increasing ginger beard may come in a close second. I would run into him for many more miles and was always impressed by his demeanor and confidence. When we were in New York State, some miles further on, he went into New York City wearing just his underpants and backpack. He even had his picture taken in Times Square with the Naked Cowboy.

My date with destiny was actually the following morning, when I planned my early morning evacuation, so to speak, with privacy in mind. The surrounding forest was particularly dense, so finding somewhere with sufficient cover should have been easy enough. However, I got a bit careless, believing that a 5:15 morning crap would rule out any chance of offending the neighbors.

Confidently finding my spot, I dug my hole in the ground, with some difficulty, and assumed the position. I was in full sumo-mode when I heard a noise and glanced to my right. There, walking through the trees, and only about 20 feet to my right rear, was Voodoo, out for her own morning constitutional. She didn't miss a step, continuing along the path, passing within a dozen feet of me. I froze on the spot, my legs spread and my pants around my ankles. With the best will in the world, it couldn't have been a pretty sight, and I was absolutely mortified that it should have been witnessed by a young woman. She said nothing, nor did I, though she couldn't possibly have missed me. My God, Stevie Wonder would have had a hard time not noticing.

Finishing up, I slowly made my way back to the shelter for breakfast, and who should be sitting at the camp table, all by herself? You've got it. The two of us had completed our business, so next on the agenda was breakfast before we left camp. I'll always be grateful that Voodoo said nothing, or indicated that she had seen me. By some distance, this was the quietest, most embarrassing breakfast of my life.

The plan for the following morning was to make my way into Port Clinton and, once more, meet up with Fran and Steve Davis. They were taking me on a tour of the nearby Yuengling Brewery, so I didn't feel too bad about a nine-mile day. Apart from burgers and pizza, beer was one of the great treats of the trail and I was really looking forward to it.

Once more, the trail was flat, though the rocks continued to test me. It is hard to imagine how wearing it is to hike over endless fields of rock, watching all the while for a white blaze, painted somewhere up ahead. Hikers were obviously slowed by these rock fields, and had to develop good balance and strong ankles to survive. Fortunately, in Pennsylvania, the weather cooperated fairly well. When rain was added to the mix, rocks could be lethal, ready to catch a hiker who let his concentration wander.

The guidebook showed quite a steep descent into Port Clinton, but it did the climb down no justice at all.

Despite its appearance, it felt like one of the steepest descents I'd made to this point, constantly jarring my knees. I thought at the time that, had it been raining, I may have camped at the top to wait until the rain stopped. I eventually made it down and, finding myself to be early for Fran and Steve, I set my sights on a late breakfast. Luckily, somebody pointed me to Port Clinton Hotel, which was about to open. I sat myself at the bar and, with no eggs available, I opted for a pint of Yuengling and probably the best burger I'd had thus far.

Steve and Fran turned up while I was stuffing my face and I could see that Steve was tempted, but he settled for a beer instead. Quite what they thought of me, and my constant piggery, I couldn't help but wonder. Despite my concerns, they seemed so taken with the romance and adventure of the trail that they remained wonderfully nonjudgmental.

The brewery was certainly worth a visit, with the free samples a high point. I noticed how out of place I felt that day among fellow members of the human race who didn't stink; wore clean, fitting clothes; and had proper jobs. It should have been my first indication that my pre-hike belief that I'd slip back into my old life after the trail in three, maybe four days, could be a bit of an underestimate. I hadn't taken temporary leave of my old life; I'd moved totally out of it.

Steve and Fran then took me to Cabela's, a vast sporting goods store, where I planned to ditch my old hiking pants. These were a rather capacious 42-inch waist and my new, svelte physique was in dire need of something a touch smaller. I initially went for 38s, but was still swamped. I couldn't imagine that I was going to be able to squeeze into 36s, but not only could I squeeze into them, they were still far too large. Settling, with incredulity on my part, for 34s, I paid up. I hadn't been that size since I was about 11 years old.

Before dropping me back at Port Clinton, Steve and Fran took me to a food store, waiting patiently as I sprinted around the store in my version of supermarket challenge. I picked up everything that had maximum fat and minimum nutritional value.

Returning to Port Clinton, I suggested that they take me to the town campsite, wait while I set up my tent, and then I would buy them dinner at the hotel for their many kindnesses. The town allowed hikers to set up in a large patch of grass right next to a road on the edge of town There was also a privy and a nearby pavilion to get out of the rain. We got to this area, just a couple of hundred yards from the hotel, and tents were strewn around somewhat haphazardly.

Having invited my friends to watch me put up my tent, I felt under pressure to live up to my promise. However, I was now sufficiently accomplished to complete the task in three or four minutes, and we were soon heading to the hotel. At this stage of the trip, I still didn't fully accept myself as a hiker, although this felt like a step towards that designation. Steve was now able to satisfy his hunger and we all ate well, with another glass or two of Yuengling to wash it all down. I loved their company, and I was glad I could repay them in a small way.

I returned to the campsite after they had left and joined my fellow hikers, who were lamenting the lack of a decent place for a quiet drink. Several of them weren't terribly keen on going to the Port Clinton Hotel, possibly due to the uniform pong emanating from us all. A local man suggested that we could get a drink at the Fire Station Clubhouse, so four of us headed that way.

The instructions were all a bit cloak and dagger. "Push the red button next to the door, tell the guy who answers that you are thirsty hikers and were wondering if you could have a drink." Fortunately, this seemed to be the magic sauce, and we were admitted without any fuss. I thought I'd buy a round of drinks and pulled out a $20 bill to pay. I figured that a private club would have higher prices than the hotel, yet three beers and a vodka-and-soda set me back the princely sum of $5.50.

A sweet day had just got sweeter by about 15 bucks.

Chapter 11: Into Palmerton

Several hikers had turned up late and, by the time I woke in the morning and got out of bed, there were people spread all over the field. I suddenly noticed young Beans, a guy I had met very early on and seen intermittently since then. He was now in tow with a young girl, Kat, which seemed a fair explanation for his lack of pace thus far. Anybody who had been hiking slower than me must have had a reason. I felt that a girl was as good a reason as any.

We chatted briefly and I left, hoping to make another 15-mile day over the rocks. It was a real grind, though there were two "Kodak" moments. One was at the Pulpit Rock, where I met a day hiker and his family who gave me a very welcome beer. The other was the Pinnacle, supposedly the best view of Pennsylvania on the A.T. Both of them were dramatic outcrops that suspended hikers over the valley far below, and each lifted my soul as I sat for a while. These moments of uninterrupted views into the distance never grew old. Even the damaging rocks beneath my feet were forgiven for a short time.

Having offered my forgiveness to the rocks, albeit temporarily, the remainder of the hike that day was rewarded by a gentle descent into Hawk Mountain Road and Eckville Shelter via a far smoother trail.

By now, one of my boots was disintegrating from the punishment it had taken to this point. My feet felt like hamburger patties. I had stopped to take a few snaps of the offending boot, along with a couple of the undamaged one, and emailed the pictures to Diane for her to work her magic.

The company, Asolo, started off by telling her that the damage was down to wear and tear. Of course, Diane was having none of it, telling the hapless customer service representative who was unlucky enough to pick up the phone to my little Rottweiler, "My husband doesn't hike with a limp, nor does he have any handicap." I'm sure the mere mention of the word "handicap" triggered something in this litigation-happy nation and it did the trick. Asolo acknowledged that a free replacement was in order, and they told Diane that it would be mailed and would meet me at Delaware Water Gap, some 70 miles down the line. Excellent and realistic customer service, aided and abetted by my tenacious wife.

What a combination.

The Eckville Shelter, at mile 1,228, was a cozy place to hang out, with a charging station for phones, a water tap which gushed out the most delectable water, a shower room, a bunkhouse, and an excellent tenting area. Unfortunately, the place was also blessed with somebody who could most charitably be described as a curmudgeonly attendant. He lived in the adjoining house and was responsible for the site.

I noticed from my phone that there was available Wi-Fi, so I asked him if I could have his password so that I could watch the extra time in a World Cup game on my iPad.

"No," was his somewhat definitive reply, though he added for clarification, "because then I'd have to give it to everybody."

While he may have seen that as a fatal flaw if he were to reveal his password, I wasn't quite getting it. However, despite my natural tendencies, I held my tongue and contented myself by listening to the game on the radio.

Miserable old sod.

That night, in my tent in a field across the road, alongside the tents of Chip and Voodoo, I stayed dry and snug with a storm raging outside. Given my naïveté in the beginning, I reflected what an excellent choice I'd made with my tent—apart from having to share it with my pack, of course. It had put up with all sorts of weather and even coped with condensation, having an inner ceiling that I'd attach at night that would channel excess moisture down into the corners and out of the tent; it worked very well.

Rain overnight always meant packing a wet tent the following morning, and that was the case the next day. Voodoo was up and out quickly, though Chip and I dawdled for no apparent reason. We commiserated with one another over our inexplicable morning tardiness. In Chip's case, he at least had the excuse of Lyme disease and his rabies shots; I was just bloody slow.

Because of my late start, I felt a little bit under the gun. The following day I was hoping to meet up with a couple of old mates at two separate spots, and I needed to put in my 13 miles to make it work.

Mark Jeffrey, a somewhat mercurial character from my old days in London, had been holidaying in the Blue Ridge Mountains, among other places, and was hoping to meet up somewhere along the way. Barry Gates, a more recent friend from Florida, had moved back to Pennsylvania a year or so before, and he was coming over to meet me as well. I always found it difficult to predict precisely where I'd be within 20 or so miles, but I had been planning these meet-ups for a few days and was on schedule.

It was another dreadfully rocky hike, and I took on substantially more lunch than usual. I needed to get the energy to put in a hard afternoon that would take me within striking distance of my planned rendezvous the following day. As often happened, the weather limited my options. I saw on my phone that a severe weather alert had been posted, and that it was heading my way. I had no alternative other than to set up my tent quickly as the rain suddenly hit me hard.

Lying in my tent, sweating profusely, with my wet pack keeping me company, the whole place got very steamy very quickly. I pushed myself into action and prepared the tent for an all-night stay. I'd been hoping the weather would pass, but it seemed established for the night. In my haste to get the tent up, I must have kept the bug net open longer than normal, because I became aware of movement on my arm as I lay there on my pad. Looking down, I saw a very large, very red spider making a run for it up my arm. Never a big fan of spiders, I whacked my own arm and squished the interloper, searching furiously for any friends that may have joined him. I'm pleased to say that I found none.

I'd set up just inside the forest, before a break in the woods that allowed for power lines to run a straight line through the terrain. My tent was in a small clearing and I woke to a foggy, calm, morning. I sat on a log to record my thoughts into my camera while I ate breakfast. Circumstances had conspired to land me at this atmospheric place, and, while I normally tried to camp near others, I felt very comfortable by myself.

Reluctantly moving on, I discovered that I'd camped just 100 yards short of an official campsite, so I followed the blue blaze down to replenish my water supply and met up again with Gizmo—who I'd met at the Fire Station in Port Clinton—and St. Rick, a fellow Brit in his thirties.

We chatted for a while, then I hiked on, only to run into some of the worst rocks so far. They were awful, with the path routed, almost viciously, through the toughest rock fields. I slowed down dramatically. Pennsylvania wasn't just attacking my boots, it was also attacking my soul.

I met up with an older guy, RW, from Chicago, who was clearly sharing my pain. We informally teamed up and tackled the infamous Knife's Edge together. Knife's Edge proved to be an ominously accurate description for these perilous rocks, with falls readily available on either side. We really paid attention as we took them on. Our careful passage notwithstanding, RW fell at one stage and cut his head, though not too badly. I, not having fallen for a while, had my thirteenth fall just before the rocks, then—as if hoping to move on from the unlucky thirteenth—had my fourteenth about ten minutes later. The first one was innocuous, softly landing me on my backside, but the second gave me a big whack on the hip and focused me once more. There is nothing like pain to bring back your focus.

I had told Mark that I'd try to be at Lehigh Furnace Gap, near Ashfield, Pennsylvania, where I hoped we could meet. Even I was a bit taken aback at just how rural the road was once I got there. As a consequence, I didn't hold out much hope that he'd be able to find it. Of course, I stayed put to see if he would. We Brits are a resilient bunch, and I knew he'd make a big effort.

Just before I reached the road, I discovered a veritable treasure trove of Trail Magic. There was note recording that the cooler was replenished every day by a man and his dog, though I guessed the dog was more of a spectator than a replenisher. I helped myself to a drink, a banana, an orange, and two donuts while I waited, feeling that eating time is never wasted time.

In the interim, a car drove up, and a young couple emerged. The two of them approached me with a free Coke which, of course, I accepted. They were part of a support team for a southbounder, who was trying to set a record time for the trip. These two were responsible for filming part of his journey. His team was hoping to raise $100,000 for an orphanage in Uganda. Once he had achieved this goal, he was moving to Uganda with his wife and child, and fostering two of the children. I couldn't think of a better example of walking the talk.

The young man and woman who approached me were also interviewing other hikers for their documentary as background, so they asked me a few questions for their film. It amused me that they would be interested in my views of the trail. I can only assume that my appearance convinced them that I knew what I was talking about.

We were just finishing up when Mark and his lovely partner, Sue, drove up, with Sue's sweet daughters. Mark and I had never been especially close in London, though we had sometimes ended up in one another's company, and we had always had a few laughs. His unpredictable behavior had often made me uneasy around him. I should record that I wasn't exactly Mr. Dependable at that time either, so my view may have been a little bit skewed. I'd never met Sue and was shocked, but delighted, that she had sawn off all of his rough edges and turned him into the great bloke who had always been there. My subsequent relative sobriety may also have enabled me to see him a lot clearer.

I was so delighted to see them. We chatted for a while and had a couple of pictures taken together. They had brought me some snacks, most of which were eaten before the day was over. Mark seemed to have thought that we could pop into a local restaurant, and have a few drinks and a nice bite to eat. However, by the time he got to me, he noted that "We're not in Kansas anymore."

I was humbled by the time and effort that people had taken in coming to see me and their continuing interest in my adventure. If that selfless detour doesn't lift your spirit, then nothing will.

I left Mark and his family and had an easy journey to my meeting place with Barry at Lehigh Gap, though I had to raise my pace in order to make the appointed time. Luckily, I ran into him as he and his son, Tyler, were hiking up a side trail that intersected with the A.T. just in front of me. Two minutes later and I would have been past his trail, and, because I didn't have any more juice in my phone, I wouldn't have had the chance to call him. Things couldn't have worked out better.

I had decided to stay the night nearby, mainly to get my clothes clean. Barry helped me find the wonderful Inn at Jim Thorpe, where both the inn and the town were named after the great Native American Olympian. We shared a coffee and a snack across the road from the Inn. Barry plied me with questions about the hike, and I tried to give him thoughtful answers.

The day taught me that, while I may have been a little blasé about hiking the Appalachian Trail by this stage, others truly saw it as an amazing achievement, even though I was less than two-thirds of the way through. It had been great to reconnect with two friends, and, for a short while, those encounters allowed me to think about something other than putting one foot in front of the other.

Alone again, I did my washing, used the Grille Room, and had a few beers and tapas before hitting the sack. I'd had a wonderfully humbling day and, although the following day held a few terrors of its own, I was ready to go again.

My Appalachian Trial II: Creaking Geezer, Hidden Flagon

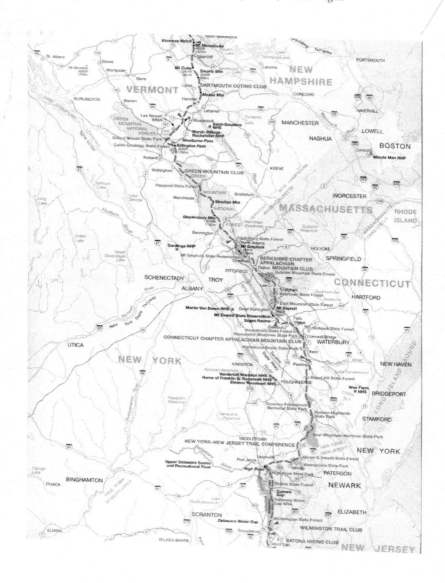

Chapter 12: Leaving Pennsylvania

I grabbed a cab the following morning and resumed my hike precisely where Barry had picked me up. That entailed crossing, and then recrossing the bridge at Lehigh Gap due to my need to hike every inch of the trail. As I wandered back over the bridge, I had the climb out of Palmerton directly in my view, rising dramatically in front of me and taunting my stamina and my nerve. This climb is reputedly the toughest stretch on the A.T. south of New Hampshire and it certainly lived up to that status. Blue Mountain near Lehigh Gap had been a Superfund site, seemingly polluted beyond redemption by a century of zinc smelting at nearby Palmerton. Amazingly, life was now growing back, and the mountain provided a stiff challenge from the start.

It wasn't that the climb lasted a terribly long time or that I reached a particularly high altitude. However, it was the first time I had been introduced to hand-over-hand climbing of any intensity. I loved it. I soon put away my poles and began hauling myself up over the rocks with a boyish enthusiasm that extended to giggling delightedly as I made progress. The rocks had white blazes to guide hikers, although I often wondered if a rock may have slipped over time, for the way indicated seemed almost impossible. However, the blazes were always correct, and I eventually concocted a path to the top. The climb was truly thrilling for me and augured well for my adventures further up the trail in New Hampshire.

I was also reminded me of my childhood vacations in Wales. My brothers and I would be unleashed by our parents to clamber on rocks near the beach all day long. We reveled in the freedom. I'd thought a lot about my brothers on this trip, and reframed in my mind our carefree, younger days when life had been so simple. I reflected, with a momentary sadness, that my own boys hadn't had such an uncomplicated existence.

At the top, the mountain opened up into an extensive ridge, with views to the countryside and small towns below. The sight even provided me with what I'd always imagined the trail to be, with long, easy ridges; expansive views; plenty of sunshine; and smooth terrain. This was the trail that had appeared in my dreams before I started my journey. Then, of course, it all went wrong.

I was loving every moment, moving along effortlessly when, suddenly and with absolutely no warning, I slipped on a patch of mud. This propelled me forward and onto my front, shoving my face into the ground. More significantly, I instinctively used my right elbow to stop myself on the rocks and that took a real thump. I struggled to my feet to see if any damage was done, fearing the worst. My elbow had a deep cut, with mud and grit embedded inside. Raising my arm to try and inspect the damage, I realized how helpful it would have been to be double-jointed at that moment. The cut was at almost the worst spot it could be in. I had been carrying a first-aid kit, so I tried to repair the damage as well as I could. Despite my best efforts, it was throbbing painfully, and all the wonderful momentum of the day had been extinguished.

To add insult to injury, I called Diane to let her know that I had fallen, had cut myself, and was a bit shaken up. In circumstances very similar to those at Duncannon a week or so earlier, I then completely missed a turn in the path while speaking with her. I wandered at least a half-mile down a hill, only to realize my mistake and have to slog back up the path.

To those of you wondering why on earth I would call my nervous Puerto Rican at that point of crisis, I can only say that you can never have been married to a Latina. They want to know everything, and an injury to their husband is like an injury inflicted upon them. They will tell you off, they will sympathize, they will implore you to be more careful, but they will want to know. I can guarantee that the moment I put the phone down, Diane would have been scouring the internet for nearby urgent care centers just in case one was needed. Being loved by a Latina has its challenges, but there is no equivocation in the depth of that love.

I eventually came to a road and stopped for lunch, feeling sorry for myself. Through the trees, I spotted a sign, on which I vaguely saw the word "resort," and wondered if this resort might have some peroxide that I could put on my cut. Temporarily postponing lunch, I wandered about 200 yards to the entrance, only to see that it was a new, developing ski resort, and that there was at least a mile walk uphill to the resort itself.

Just then, as so often happened on the trail, a guy in a truck pulled up and offered to run me to the top. His name was Jethro, and he was an engineer working on the project. He drove me to the top, led me to the first-aid room, found peroxide, sprayed the wound, gave me several bandages, then ran me back to where I had stopped for lunch. Once again, the kindness of others was there when I least expected it, yet needed it the most.

I was still sitting there, munching on my wrap, when he skidded to a halt ten minutes later. He jumped out to give me back my Nalgene bottle, which must have fallen out when I shoved my pack into the back of his truck. I thanked him once more and we parted as friends.

While still eating lunch, I was joined at the roadside by Wilderness Hawk and his wife, Cinnamon Girl, along with their friend, Tee Bird. They were a very engaging group, and wanted a drink, which was always fine by me. I joined them when they spotted another guy in a truck who seemed content to take us to find a bar. Unfortunately, we were still in a very rural area, so the best we could find was an ice cream shop. Ice cream is a poor alternative when you are hunting for alcohol, though an acceptable replacement when you're a hungry hiker.

Getting back to the trailhead seemed just as easy, as two of the shop's customers stepped up to drive us back. I spent the next three hours hiking with my new friends. I thoroughly enjoyed their company, and would have gladly spent some more time with them. However, I was eager to get to the Leroy Smith Shelter, so I moved ahead while the three of them took a break.

At Smith Gap Road, just three or four miles before the shelter, I ran into my first Trail Magic for a couple of days, gratefully gulping down a bottle of Powerade to help me through the rest of the day.

Though I didn't know it at the time, Tee Bird was going to play a significant part in the end of my journey, but that wouldn't be for many more miles.

The following morning, my arm was starting to worry me a little, particularly in light of my brush with cellulitis in late May. I looked online for an urgent care facility to put my mind—and elbow—at ease. The throbbing had, if anything, increased, and I knew I shouldn't leave it. Injury had put paid to many a hike. I would have hated to have had my journey curtailed because of an unattended, fairly minor injury.

Fortunately, there was a facility in Wind Gap, which was a couple of miles off the trail at PA33, which, in turn, was just a four-mile hike that morning. I thought I'd easily be able to grab a hitch into town, but the place at which the trail cut across PA33 made hitching, at best hazardous and, at worst, downright suicidal. Cars screamed around a bend and over a ridge. They were beyond me before their drivers could even contemplate stopping, so I bit the bullet and walked two miles into town.

The doctor decided, given the earlier incident with my canine adversary, to treat the wound as if it might develop into cellulitis. Consequently, he gave me the same awful antibiotics, and bound the wound far more carefully than I had.

Never one to miss the eating opportunities inherent within a town, I soon found a pizza joint nearby and indulged myself in this guilt-free pleasure once more.

I was able to hitch back to the trail, and immediately ran into St. Rick again. We hiked the rest of the day together. He improved my pace, and we reached Kirkridge Shelter, after a 14-mile day. Given my detour, which had lasted about three hours, I was delighted with the progress. I was also just six miles short of Delaware Water Gap, which marked the end of Rocksylvania.

The Maine sisters and J-Rex were leaving as we got there. They told us that there was a tenting area with a great view just a third of a mile ahead. We considered leaving and seeing if there was space, but in the end we stayed and had a quiet evening.

While I was rarely unhappy with a quiet evening, the following morning quickly demonstrated that I had made a poor choice by staying close to the shelter. The campsite had plenty of room, with a field that could have accommodated 50 tents. There was a wide, open view of the valley below. It was simply gorgeous. On the principle of "some you win," this was one I had lost, though it was a loss that I was about to reverse in the best way possible.

I started the descent from Mount Minsi, past the beautiful view from Lookout Rock, into Delaware Water Gap. I was very pleased that Pennsylvania had finished beating me up. While I knew that the terrain wouldn't change immediately, I'd heard from others that the rocks, which had been the bane of our lives for the past two or three weeks, would start to ease off.

My feet would have a breather before the rigors of New England.

My new boots were ready for me to pick up at the post office and I was idly thinking about those when I ran into Sugar Mama, or Sug, for short. When I say I ran into her, it was more a case of her Trail Magic set-up completely blocking my path. Sug had everything: hot food, fruit, drinks, supplies, and all of it was free to hikers. I've seen less well-stocked convenience stores. Her daughter had tried the hike in 2012, and Sug was so grateful for the support that her daughter had received from fellow hikers that she does this to give back to those also thru-hiking. We had quite a party, sitting around, eating and chatting, while the lovely Sug fussed over us like a mother hen.

I still had to pick up my food drop and my new boots, so I reluctantly left after about an hour. The post office turned out to be nearer than I had thought and, less than ten minutes later, I was standing in my new size 14s, pushing still more food into my two food bags. I was nearly 1,300 miles into the hike and, while my old boots were on their last legs, so to speak, they had carried me without a single blister. I fervently hoped for the same result with my new ones.

A quick limeade in an Haitian-fusion restaurant enabled me to recharge my phone and I was off into New Jersey. I was hiking up and out of town, hopeful that the rocks would soon fade away. I should also mention that I recorded my sixteenth fall of the trip and my fourth in about three days.

One oddity about my long stay in Pennsylvania was that, despite its reputation for plenty of wildlife, I had seen not a single snake along the way. There had been plenty before this state, and would be several later, yet not one, amongst all the rocks that I had crossed, in Pennsylvania. Several hikers doubted that this was possible, but, unless I had been suddenly struck blind for the previous 230 miles, it was another unexpected outcome in a journey of unexpected outcomes.

Chapter 13: New Jersey

While I was grateful to be leaving Pennsylvania, I knew that New Jersey wasn't going to entirely rock-free. Of course, this turned out to be the case. That said, there was an immediate, distinct improvement. The profile of the climb out of Delaware Water Gap didn't look too bad in my guidebook, though I found it to be quite challenging, particularly in the heat of the day. I'm also sure that wearing in my new boots may have had something to do with it.

I eventually got to the top and followed the trail until it reached the magnificent Sunfish Pond. The southernmost glacial pond on the A.T., it was a stunning sight to suddenly encounter.

The warmth and the stillness of the day enhanced the beauty of the pond, as I sat at the edge, in silence. After my contemplation, I moved on and the trail circled the pond. The rocks provided me with further difficulties, though this effort gave me the bonus of a very special view for the 40 or so minutes it took me to ultimately move away from this dramatic feature.

With my new boots behaving impeccably, I made good time for the rest of the afternoon, and got to the Mohican Outdoor Center after a 17-mile day. Immediately before the road leading to the Center there was a small wooden bridge that crossed a tiny stream, proudly announcing that I had passed 1,300 miles.

At the Center, I paid a few bucks to pitch my tent in my own little spot, boasting a picnic table and a bit of privacy. I found myself next to a young couple, Mark and Sarah, who were out for a two-day camping trip. They invited me to join them for some real food. Following night after night of pasta and rice, it was heavenly. We spoke quietly about both the trail and my hike until it was almost pitch dark. When I was with other hikers, I tended to forget how unusual this adventure was to others, and I always enjoyed sharing my experiences with day hikers.

A few spots away from me were Tee Bird, along with Wilderness Hawk and Cinnamon Girl, so I felt among friends. I allowed myself to drift ahead to Katahdin. I had tried to keep that thought out of my mind but somehow, passing 1,300 miles indicated that I was considerably past halfway. I spent an introspective ten minutes before drifting off to sleep imagining the summit. I actively banished this thought the next morning, with the realization that I still had another 900 miles to go, and the toughest stuff still to come. That said, with Katahdin in my mind, I slept as peacefully as I had for some weeks.

I had shifted up another gear.

I still needed my sporting fixes, so I set myself an 18-mile goal the following morning. I wanted to reach Culvers Gap by the end of the day, a Saturday. I'd chosen a motel and intended to indulge myself the following morning by watching the last round of the Open Golf Championship from the U.K. The five-hour time difference would allow me to see the finish, then hike out just after lunch. I'd be back in the woods, at a shelter, before the sun set.

I hadn't really considered what the hike would be like that day. New Jersey is named "The Garden State," but I had only seen the industrial areas from my time living in New York. I guess I'd imagined that title to be self-deprecating, but it wasn't. I discovered a beauty I hadn't expected in New Jersey. The unadulterated glory of it all took me unawares, the rocks notwithstanding. I was completely unprepared for the wilderness and beauty that I saw that day. I walked along a spectacular ridge that had constant views of the greenery and distant scenery to the right, with regular, though not too taxing, ups and downs that always kept my interest. It is often worthwhile to have your preconceived ideas shattered, particularly when the shattering is positive.

At Culvers Gap, I was greeted by the welcome sight of Stoke's Steakhouse and Pub. The name alone was enough to get me drooling in anticipation, and the place itself didn't disappoint. Eagerly offloading my backpack, I tucked into a few beers, a burger, and some pie along with about a dozen other hikers.

I was keen to get to my room for the night, so, after this calorific blowout, I called that night's landlord and he came to pick me up at the pub. He had made a good start but things began to go downhill from there.

There ought to be a law that, when a motel or a hotel advertises that it has Wi-Fi, then it should have a working version. The fact that it may work somewhat intermittently in the office of the motel doesn't cut it for me. I need it to operate in my room, not fade away with every tentative step I take towards my room. While I accept that a place that charges $41.45 a night isn't going to boast every modern convenience, the rash statement that it has Wi-Fi should be at least passably accurate.

You are probably getting the gist of my complaint that this particular motel both boasted, though lacked, anything that could conceivably be regarded as working Wi-Fi. As luck would have it, the owner told me that it always worked. Apparently, I was the only person who had ever been unable to get access to it. I'm afraid that my disbelieving look went right over his head, as he fiddled about with knobs and dials as if to effect some magical outcome.

Nevertheless, there I was on Sunday morning, trying to watch both the German Formula One Grand Prix and the last day of the Open Golf Championship.

There are few things that can rile me, but I think that I found one that day. Every 45 or so seconds—just as Rory McIlroy was about to take a putt, or Lewis Hamilton was on the verge of pulling off a thrilling passing maneuver—the screen on my iPad would freeze. A few seconds later it would reset, and the action had moved on, not unreasonably, without me. My language became increasingly earthy and loud, so much so that I just turned off the tablet, checked out, and got the owner to shuttle me back to the pub from the previous day. He was still incredulous that I had failed to get onto his system. I just said, "Yeah, funny how that goes," then ignored him. Git.

The pub actually had a working system, so I got online sitting on a bench outside until it opened. I snagged a seat underneath the TV, with the golf on, and spent several carefree hours eating like a greedy hog and cheering Rory to victory.

Unfortunately, this didn't do much for my hiking that day. I limited my ambition to the first shelter—Gren Anderson—at only three miles away, because it was the only shelter that offered water for about 15 miles. As you'd imagine, getting water was one of the critical reasons for being at a shelter, and New Jersey had been a little lacking in that regard. Fortunately, several trail angels continued to go out of their way to provide water at road intersections, so hikers were getting by.

However, a water source quickly became a top priority when planning the day in this state.

As I say, it was only supposed to be a three-mile hike, but I managed to turn it into more like double that distance when I completely missed a change of direction. These changes were always indicated by double white blazes, but I breezed right past them. I ended up going down a precipitous descent that landed me on a road which shouldn't have been there, according to my guide. It is a salutary experience to come to a road that doesn't appear to exist: you feel like you've stumbled into an alternate universe. I knew I'd gone wrong. I also knew that I'd have to slog back uphill just to get to my missed double blazes. Eventually, I found them and got back into top gear, only to completely miss the blue blaze that indicated the shelter, hiking at least a mile past the entrance. Realizing I'd messed up yet again—a realization that incorporated considerably harsher language than "messed up,"—I had to turn round, wasting more miles and calories in getting to the right place.

I was thoroughly ticked off when I eventually got to the shelter. The place was utterly deserted, which meant that I couldn't even shout at anybody. I didn't fancy cooking, so I made myself a wrap and a cup of tea, only to spill the entire cup into my lap. Not having anybody to shout at, I made do with the forest, and unleashed a few choice words. Shouting at trees can be marvelously restorative, though it does nothing to ease the stinging of your throbbing privates. After my outburst, it was eerily quiet. I started to prepare myself for a lonesome night, with the entire site to choose from in which to pitch my tent. A few people came in a while later, but just to collect water, and I was soon alone again.

As a consequence—and I'm convinced it was because I was alone—I needed to use the privy at about 3:30 a.m., and so donned my camp shoes, my fleece, my underpants, and my nightlight. I must have looked like Wee Willie Winkie, from the English nursery rhyme, carefully padding over the rocks, trying to identify the path to the privy. With nobody else around, the darkness and the quiet ate into me, and I made it back to my tent, now fully alert and listening to every noise that assaulted my ears for the next hour or so. Thankfully, there were no incidents, so I fell back into a deep sleep, before gloomily waking, drinking my coffee, and chomping on my oatmeal in silence.

I was on the trail at 7:45, pushing for a 20-mile day, because I needed to make up for the measly three miles recorded the day before. The goal was to get to the High Point State Park HQ for lunch, charge my phone at the office, then move on to Unionville, where the mayor was allowing thru-hikers to stay in a local park.

Everything worked out as planned; the state park even had free sodas, always a bonus. The hiking was still fairly tricky, with several rocks to slow my progress. However, I often found that the further I planned to travel, the easier it was. If I knew that I needed to do ten miles before lunch, then ten miles after lunch, that seemed to be more achievable than having no plan or aiming low.

Earlier, about three hours into the day, I saw my ninth bear and my first in New Jersey. The bear suddenly ran at an angle away from me, through the undergrowth to my right, its thick fur gleaming in the intermittent sunlight. Bears didn't worry me now and each sighting was a bonus thrillingly received and enjoyed.

I made the road into Unionville by about 6:30 that evening and walked towards the town, which was less than half a mile off the trail. Unionville is actually located in New York, so I was crossing into my ninth state, albeit temporarily. I wouldn't leave New Jersey for New York permanently for another 20 or so miles.

Passing one of the gardens along the road into town, I spotted Spider, one of the guys I'd been hiking with in recent days. He was sitting in a chair, talking with the owner as if they were lifelong buddies. The owner, Blake, motioned me to join them and I could tell straightaway that he was several Jack Daniels on the wrong side of the optimum amount. Nonetheless, Blake was perfectly affable, introducing me to his wife, Joy, and Blake Junior, then dividing their grilled meat into five servings, as opposed to their previously anticipated three. Generosity seemed to come to hikers out of all proportion to the normal actions of folks. I was humbled once more.

When we'd had our fill of steak and chicken, Spider and I left Blake and his family and made it to the park, where several old friends were already set up. These included Naturally Hob, along with his wife, Chickadee, plus Dos Lekis, Yeti Legs, Flea, and several others, including a newcomer, Rogue, who I'd met earlier in the day.

There was a very cordial atmosphere in the park, with all of us grateful to the mayor for such a good facility, boasting a porta potty, free drinking water, and free tent sites. Sadly, that gratitude didn't extend to respecting the public nature of the park. The youngsters called a "safety meeting," inviting the older hikers as well, before they sat around strumming a ukulele and relaxing fragrantly once more. I probably sound like a bit of an old fart—a charge to which I'm delighted to plead guilty—but I feel that was thoughtless. Use of the park for future hikers could have been jeopardized. Nothing happened, though it could have, and I was disappointed in some of my fellow travelers for the first time. We were privileged to have been able to stay in the park; exercising some judgment at this stage would have been appropriate.

The park cleared out quickly in the morning, and, as usual, I was the last to leave. I charged my phone at the convenience store across from the park, ate two donuts, and had two coffees, all of which was after I'd eaten my regular breakfast. I retraced my steps, listening to a podcast on my phone. Once more, I totally missed the trailhead, going a good quarter of a mile past. Cursing myself again, a reasonably regular occurrence in the previous couple of days, I got back on track at last.

The 20-miler I'd put in the previous day had sapped me and, in conjunction with some very tricky rocks, I stopped for lunch after only five miles. My day completely reset. I had intended to get to the lusciously named Wawayanda Shelter, some 17 miles away. Instead, I went for the church hostel in Vernon, New Jersey, and an 11-mile day.

For a suggested donation of $10, I got access to a shower, a laundry room, a shared recreation room, and a tent site. I found several fellow hikers, but only one, Senator, wanted to go for sushi at a nearby Japanese restaurant. He had worked for a senator in the Florida State Senate, and was a very smart young man. As an added bonus, he was also an extremely funny guy; I greatly enjoyed his company. After the sushi, neither of us took much convincing to go for a Blizzard ice cream at Dairy Queen. Guilt-free eating was going to be a tough habit to kick on my return to civilization.

However, the day wasn't over. I showered and laundered my clothes back at the hostel and we had a late visit by a lovely older couple, Dori and Tom. They asked if three of us would like to join them in the morning for a swim in their local lake, followed by breakfast, then return to the trail. Spider, Voodoo, and I shot up our hands, so we arranged to be ready for 7:15 the following day.

The three of us were ready on time, and Dori came to collect us. She took us to her picturesque community, giving us a guided tour along the way. She was a charming hostess. The lake was enticing, though unveiling my new, fat-free body was a bit embarrassing. Mind you, I figured that Voodoo had already seen me squatting in the woods with my pants around my ankles, so a skinny bloke in swimming trunks, with loose skin where his gut used to be, shouldn't be too unnerving for her.

We all swam for about 20 minutes, then headed back to Tom and Dori's log cabin home. Ever the teacher—which had been her profession—Dori gave everybody a task while putting together a wonderful breakfast that included eggs, bacon, toast, fruit, and yogurt. We were back on the trail by 10:30, with our gratitude on overload.

I had gotten used to hiking on my own, but Voodoo, Spider, and I started the day together, and eventually ended the day together. We also met up with the Maine Sisters—Navigator and Toots—along the way. Once more, the rocks slowed everybody's pace, allowing us to trek as a team. It was the largest group I had hiked with since starting, and I enjoyed the camaraderie.

Towards the end of the day, we passed out of New Jersey and were now properly in New York. There was a dividing line painted unceremoniously on a rock on the trail, so we all posed for selfies.

New Jersey had been a revelation for me, with the rocks less demanding than in Pennsylvania. The hiking was still tricky and always afforded distant, beautiful views. Having been to Newark a few times, I think my surprise was understandable, and—if you know Newark—considerably understated.

Chapter 14: Into New York

At around this time, I let my group go ahead of me as I tried, fairly unsuccessfully, to join a conference call with the charity in which I'm involved. By the time the call was over, the sun was rapidly going down, so I chased down my group, eventually catching them at NY17A. They were heading for Bellvale Creamery, a local ice cream shop located a few hundred yards from the trail.

We each demolished huge banana splits, an outrageously tasty bargain at $6, then looked around for somewhere to camp. I investigated a virtually empty parking lot just 50 yards away, up a small hill. While there were no signs regarding camping, we wondered if it might be a teeny bit illegal. Given the paucity of options we went ahead and set up anyway. The rain was coming, so we figured that might work in our favor if somebody decided that we shouldn't have been there. By now, I could summon the pathetic-loser look at will.

Despite the rain and fairly lively winds during the night, we were undisturbed. Morning came with the wind still dancing all about us, though the rain had moved on. I got out fairly early and hiked alone for a while, running into a few new and one or two old faces on the way. I was aware that I was running low on certain supplies and, with my speed still moderately glacial over some of the more persistent rocks, I asked Diane to book me a motel room in Southfields after only about 11 miles.

I'd just spoken with the cab company that was going to pick me up, telling its dispatcher that I'd be at the pick-up point in five minutes. I turned a corner, and was confronted by as steep a descent over sharp rocks as I had seen to this point. In my effort not to miss the shuttle, I started to hurry and slipped, catapulting my legs into the air and falling, head first, and completely upside down, to the rocks below. This took place in an instant. I screamed, like a child, as if to mask the inevitable pain, and probable death, when it came. My normal, sunny optimism failed me at that moment. Luckily, I managed to avoid smashing my head on the rocks, coming to rest totally inverted, with my pack lurching up and over my shoulders. I was relatively unhurt. There were a few scrapes and the odd laceration on my arms and legs, with a developing bruise already on my upper arm. I managed to get myself the right way up and continued, rather gingerly, and distinctly chastened, on my way.

At the bottom, my shuttle driver was waiting for me. As if to explain being late, I shared my recent incident with him. He looked at me, shrugged, pursed his lips, and put his head to one side. While he said nothing, he had that look on his face that said, *What do you bloody expect, clambering about on those rocks at your age?* I had to concede that he had a valid point.

Later that night in my room, feeling a touch sorry for myself, I ordered Chinese takeout. It was a rare luxury, and came with a fortune cookie that could not have been more apposite.

"Keep on, keeping on."

Just when I needed it, as so often happened before, the trail had provided.

I woke the following morning, expecting to find my entire body on fire or as stiff as a board. Fortunately, it was neither and nothing was broken, apart from my pride. I called a cab for 9 o'clock, and got straight back into it.

I was entering Harriman State Park and it was absolutely beautiful, with rolling, gentle, forested hills, crossed by a wider, well-maintained path that really warmed my soul. The pain, indeed, the fear, of the previous day had got to me, so this was a perfect way to get back on the horse.

Then I came to the Lemon Squeezer, so-called because of the curious rock formation that forces hikers to squeeze their already emaciated frames through a very narrow gap. When I saw it, I wondered if my heavier, earlier self could even have made it. I took my pack off and shoved it onto a rock, then climbed out of the gap, only to see J-Rex and her boyfriend, Max, coming along behind. I took their packs while they climbed up. Thinking that it hadn't been too bad, we saw the next part, which was an abrupt wall about eight to ten feet high.

Max climbed up, discovering several tiny hand and footholds that I hadn't seen. We pushed J-Rex's pack and mine up to him, then pulled ourselves up. I couldn't help thinking at the time that I would have been unable to do this had I been alone. As I've recorded before, I preferred to hike by myself, at my pace, yet, with the tougher New England states coming up, I wondered whether or not a hiking partner might be sensible.

I didn't know it at the time, but I would eventually get three partners.

Max and J-Rex were spending a couple of days together on the trail, having been parted for some months. Seeing the two of them together impacted me more than I expected and I lost my early impetus. It often happened—normally when I least expected it—that a word, a moment, or even a close relationship, would take the wind from my sails. I'd miss Diane, my home, and my life. With such fluctuating moods, I started to understand why some days I was able to do 20 miles quite easily, while other days I struggled to make ten.

Eager to move on and find some water, I eventually found some at Beechy Bottom Brook. A few miles later, at Seven Lakes Drive, I decided that I'd had enough for the day. I had intended to go up and over Bear Mountain, then stay at Bear

Mountain Inn, for an 18-mile day, but I was done. I justified stopping as I'd slightly exceeded my 13.3 mile target. Justifying my mileage became a bit of an obsession for me during these middle miles.

At Seven Lakes Drive, with only three-quarters of a liter of water left in my Nalgene, I set up my tent just off the road. I made sure that I was out of sight because I wasn't supposed to camp there. Diane was never crazy about me camping alone, but I enjoyed the occasional night like this. The solitude allowed me to think completely uninterrupted. Given the limited water that remained, I had a wrap for dinner to preserve some for coffee the following morning.

That night, at around 1:30 a.m., I was woken by the sound of coyotes baying, presumably at the moon. While I always felt irrationally safe in my tent, noises like this, with nobody around, tended to make the next 30 or so minutes a touch uncomfortable. After a few more yelps and, to my mind, blood-curdling screams, the little blighters decided to give it a rest and I drifted off.

For breakfast the next day I limited myself to coffee and a Snickers. I had about four miles to go—up and over Bear Mountain—before getting a chance to refill my water bottle once more. I always found this water uncertainty to be a bad start to the day. I was expecting the climb to be taxing, and I knew I'd start offloading liquid through every orifice within seconds.

Fortunately, the hike was much easier than I had thought, resembling, in my imagination, a walk along the ramparts of Sauron's castle, in Mordor, from Tolkien's *Lord of the Rings* trilogy, or something out of an Indiana Jones movie. While I loved it, the trail seemed to be less wild and more manicured to my eyes. The thought was compounded when I came upon an older, quite refined, Chinese couple near the top, having breakfast on a neatly laid-out mat. Quite what they thought about my disheveled appearance they kept to themselves. When they found that I was a thru-hiker, the old man very sweetly, and with much solemnity, presented me with a pack of blueberries. I gratefully accepted them and wolfed them all down when I was out of sight. Some proprieties need to be observed.

I had assumed I was at the top but, in fact, there was still additional, though no less manicured, climbing to get there. At the very top were restrooms and soda machines—more Disney World than Mordor—so I drank a Powerade and bought some water to top up my bottle. Everything on Bear Mountain is done with the day hiker in mind. It is the busiest mountain on the entire trail, and the path is tremendously well-managed and -maintained.

The stairs down—over 700 of them—were strenuous, but magnificent. At the bottom, the trail took me through a park, with families preparing food for a big day out. I refilled with water once more, then strolled slowly through the park. I was trying out my pathetic and hungry face this time, in the hope that they'd throw me a hot dog. They must see hikers all day long, because I wasn't even thrown a bone. I clearly wasn't as pathetic and hungry as I thought I was. I made a mental note to perfect the look.

Through the park, the white blazes led me to the entrance of the zoo, and I arrived just before opening time at 10 o'clock. I hurried through, though the lady who let me in found me some peanut butter crackers, so the look must at least have worked on her.

Having seen wildlife where it belonged made me reluctant to watch any of the many animals caged for my viewing pleasure, but I couldn't resist stopping at the bear compound. There were two of them, apparently black bears, but both with dirty brown coats and slow, lumbering gaits. They were nothing like the bears I'd seen on my trip. It may have taken me a while to see any, but the ones I'd been lucky enough to encounter were full of life, foraging and climbing, with a vitality that was in stark contrast to the prisoners in front of me. I'd had another moment of clarity in six months of such revelations.

Leaving the zoo, the trail then crossed the Hudson River via a bridge, and I was at the lowest point on the entire trail, at 124 feet above sea level. Before I could start my climb after the bridge, I passed 1,400 miles, without any discernible marker.

The climb back up the other side of the Hudson was extremely steep. Huffing and puffing my way along, I ran into a trail maintainer, out for a day hike. He obviously wanted to sample the fruits of his considerable labor. We fell into a companionable hike together for a couple of miles before he went off in a different direction to return to his car. I always enjoyed meeting these selfless people who volunteered to make my day better. I knew that I and my fellow hikers were aware of the enormous debt that we owed them. It isn't too much to say that without these dedicated people, there would be no trail. They make the difference between being able to hike the trail and there being no trail to hike.

US9 had a great deli and, as I'd already decided to stay at the Graymoor Friary less than a mile further on, I got stuck into a real, chunky, fat-filled New York sandwich, which was basically a heart attack in waiting—with fries on the side in case the sandwich didn't get me. The deli had stools and tables and these were filled with ravenous hikers chatting about their day while chomping on huge plates of food. For me, whenever I think of New York since this trip, those delis located on or near the trail come to mind first, as opposed to the Statue of Liberty or Times Square. I guess that reflects a changed perspective.

Just beyond the deli, after a brief return to the forest, I came to a road. That led me to the Friary, where I was directed to the ball field. This was an open tenting site for hikers and, despite the recent ingestion of unhealthy food, I ordered a pizza.

I should say at this point, by the way, that I was still losing weight. I was now down to 185 pounds, from my original 245 pounds. I seemed to be losing weight at a more catastrophic rate than my peers, but I found it almost impossible to increase my calorific input. I should also say that I started to ship in peanut butter on an almost industrial scale at around this time, often demolishing an entire jar in a day. My additional fat intake allowed me to return to Diane in a slightly less emaciated form, putting 10 pounds back on and weighing in at 195 pounds. She wasn't thrilled with how I looked at that weight, so I was glad that she only saw my 185-pound look in the odd photograph.

Back at the Friary, there were many hikers around the field. We all wandered from tent to tent, chatting amiably until the light faded, then settled in for the night.

In the morning, idly sipping my coffee and spooning down my oatmeal, I spotted an older black guy, No Pain, so I wandered over for a chat. He had slung his hammock just away from the field in the woods. He told me that he had done the trail several times before, and entertained me with several stories of the changing generations he had met over the years on the A.T. No Pain admitted to being a loner and looked regretfully sad to me. He shared with me that he had a family "somewhere," though he didn't seem in any great hurry to re-connect with them. Given my rather fractured relationship with my younger son, I felt for him. He stayed in my thoughts for quite a while after that one occasion when we met.

I set off with the RPH shelter—originally, Ralph's Peak Hiker Cabin—as an 18-mile target. I was going well until the heavens opened, and I got completely drenched. I tried to wring out my socks every twenty minutes or so, but I kept hiking, drying out as the sun broke through, with damp feet plaguing me all day.

The terrain was excellent, with few rocks, several flattish areas, and hardly any steep climbs. One exception was the stupendous ascent to Shenandoah Mountain, followed by a glorious walk across the rocks. In much the same way that the beauty of New Jersey had surprised me, New York seemed to have similarly upended previous perceptions.

On Shenandoah Mountain, I came upon the September 11 Memorial Flag painted on the rocks. I'd read about this and expected it to be cheesy, but it was a stark reminder of man's inhumanity to man. I sat there for fully an hour before moving on, thinking of how that day affected me, 13 years previously.

September 11, 2001, marked the 15-year anniversary of my split from my first wife and, given that I had subsequently split with my second wife in July 2001, I was preoccupied with all things divorce. I was dating an inappropriately younger woman at the time, and chose to mark the day with a few drinks with her that lunchtime. My girlfriend had to return to work at around 2 p.m., which was 9 a.m. in New York, and I headed back to my office.

We had a TV constantly on in the office, and everybody was huddled around watching what seemed to have been a tragic accident some 20 minutes before, 3,000 miles away in New York City. Within seconds of walking back into the office, the second plane appeared on the screen. We all watched, silently, and in horrific realization, as it was deliberately rammed into the second tower. In that instant, we all knew instinctively that our lives had changed. We continued to watch, an ocean away, as America fell into the fear and paranoia that it has still to fully shrug off.

I was due to fly to New York the following week, and had arranged several appointments in the World Trade Center.

However, my second wife was under the impression that I was there that day. She was at work and, hearing the news, panicked when she thought I was in the towers. She called my office, more frantic than somebody who had previously seemed content to be as far away as possible from me should really be. Assured that I was standing in London and not New York, her previous bitterness returned, and we resumed antagonizing one another. I always joked after that call that she was just worried because we hadn't finalized our financial settlement at the time, though I know her concern was real and heartfelt.

Sitting on Shenandoah Mountain, at the U.S. flag, I thought of those who had been there that day. I knew that my 9/11 story was a trivial one. Others had suffered horrors from which they would never recover. Having decided that God wasn't there earlier in the trip, I had a quiet word with Him, alone on that mountain, sitting quietly by that flag, just in case He might be listening.

He and I never spoke again.

Chapter 15: Out of New York

The shelter was just a short downhill hop of a couple of miles from the flag and I limped soggily in, meeting up with the regular combination of friends old and new. As usual, I was pretty much last to the shelter, so I had to set up my tent with expected rain, thunder, and lightning as added attractions to look forward to.

Before turning in for the evening, I started a rather stilted conversation with a young Japanese guy over dinner. He was a section hiker, by himself, with nobody speaking to him. I had learned a few Japanese words in my business life, so I tried to make conversation. Unfortunately, being able to ask the way to Tokyo Station, knowing the word for telephone—*denwa bango*, in case you were wondering—and asking my cab driver to return me to the Hotel Okura, didn't come in terribly handy on that damp evening.

Despite living in Queens, the young lad's English was very basic, though considerably less basic than my Japanese, so we couldn't have much of a chat. I eventually gave up the ghost and went to my tent, with the weather growing more ominous every second. The weather behaved as expected and, the following morning as I was preparing to leave, my Japanese friend reciprocated, speaking to me with difficulty. As I've said before, it could get lonely on the trail, so I understood why he was making the effort.

I gave him my few Japanese words and we laughed at each other's efforts. Once I set off, he was soon behind me, trying to chat once more. Eventually, I stopped for a rest and he moved on. My plan was to get to the strangely named Telephone Pioneers Shelter, about 17 miles away, although my first port of call was going to be another deli, at NY52, after just five miles.

The terrain, like much of this state, was challenging in terms of ups and downs, though not too extensive, while the rocks often served more to decorate the trail than to impede progress. I'd become a real fan of New York hiking and was loving the morning.

I'd told my Japanese friend about the deli, and he said that he would see me there. Once I got there, he was buying up the shop, with all sorts of goodies to cram into not only his mouth but also his food bag. As we sat companionably outside, shoveling food into our faces, I asked him why he was in the U.S. and how he had got here.

He explained to me that he had been a worker at the nuclear reactor plant in Fukushima and that, on the fateful day of that devastating quake, he had been working in a separate building nearby. He had managed to get out quickly, but his home was in a dangerously contaminated area, so he and his family had to move to safety that very day. He also shared with me that, while it was a terrible day, he had come to terms with it, and regarded it as an opportunity to come to America.

I then asked him if he had a trail name. He replied that nobody had named him thus far. I couldn't help it, as my darkly British humor beat out my American political correctness. I gave him the name of Tsunami. To my intense delight, and equal relief, he laughed uproariously and graciously accepted the name.

That was two trail names to my credit. I hoped this one would stick.

Several hikers were also coming by the deli, so I hung around for about an hour and a half, grazing relentlessly with my friends, before heading out once more. The expression "chewing the fat" had never held such a double meaning for me prior to this trip.

On leaving the deli, I checked my emails and found one from a lawyer. He promised me another opportunity to defray my costs for a few hours' work, so I found a hotel and access to Wi-Fi, finishing my hike for the day at that point, with only five miles under my belt. I put up with the bitter disappointment of not reaching my goal by submitting an invoice for about $2,000. That made me feel a whole lot better.

The excitement of this cash infusion clearly upset my sense of location, and I wasted 20 minutes the following morning trying to find where I'd left the trail the previous day. The cab driver dropped me where I thought he'd picked me up, but I couldn't find the entrance to the trail on the other side of the road for the life of me. You might have thought I'd have developed a nose for this sort of thing by now, but I'm afraid not. Unless I had a white blaze beckoning me on, I was hopelessly lost.

More from a process of elimination than anything else, I found my way back onto the trail, and that got me on my way by 9 o'clock. Starting behind my own schedule would often make me struggle for the rest of the day. That proved to be the case here. I was planning to get to Kent, Connecticut, by the next evening, where I would meet dear friends, Brian and Dee. My late start made me adjust my target for the day. I was heading for the Appalachian Trail Metro North train station, the only station on the A.T. By stopping there, I knew that I'd be giving myself a 19-miler the next day, but when I was struggling, I often had to accept the fact and modify my plans accordingly.

The terrain continued to delight me, with wonderful hiking that established New York as my favorite state on the trail to that point. The rocks were never too onerous and the paths were well groomed, while the climbs continued to challenge without defeating me. I should also say that, despite losing all my fat, I'd retained a lot of strength, and was hiking better all the time. I'm sure that the struggles, when they came, were more about my state of mind than about my physical abilities.

Early on that day, I came upon the imaginatively named Von Trapps. They were a family of five from Canada who were hiking the whole trail. They were dad, Toe Salad; mum, Fimby; a calm daughter of about 13, Padawan; a younger, intense girl, Tenacious Bling; and a cheerful young boy, Otter. They were having a wonderful adventure together, brimming with positivity, while retaining a sensible realism. I enjoyed chatting with them while they were filling their water bottles and eventually moved on, musing about them as I did.

The problem was that I couldn't get the Von Trapps, or, more specifically, the Julie Andrews songbook, out of my head. I started to sing, somewhat louder than my voice should ever be heard, "Doe, a deer, a female deer, ray, a drop of golden sun," and so on. I was just blasting out the bit where Julie Andrews and the kids jump up and down on the stairs in time to the music "Doe, mee, mee, mee, so, so," when I realized that I hadn't spotted a white blaze for a while and that I was completely lost. I stopped, with my hands raised, as if in submission, looked left, then right, like an idiot cartoon character, called out "Bollocks," to nobody in particular, though with a certain amount of venom, and turned round. I retraced my steps until I spotted a white blaze after about a quarter of a mile and resumed my hike. Following this unexpected interlude, I contented myself with "Climb Every Mountain," and paid more attention.

Near the end of the day's hike, just before I reached the station, I was lucky enough to run into some more Trail Magic, always a terrific component to any day. There were goodies galore but, to be honest, the thing that made me most pleased was when the trail angel started recounting who had gone through. She said, "…and there was this nice Japanese boy called Tsunami." I couldn't help but smile to myself.

Trail name number two, in the books.

Right next to the station, there was a local garden center that allowed hikers to tent on its grounds, charge their phones, get water from a spigot, and use the restroom. Whilst this wasn't exactly akin to a suite at the Ritz, when you can't take life's luxuries for granted you'd be amazed how welcome they are when you find them.

Having taken a couple of idiot-grin selfies on the station platform, I got to the garden center at about 5 o'clock, and, after finding where to pitch my tent, chatted with the guy on duty in the center to see if there was a better alternative to the deli down the road. While I could find no fault with any of the delis in New York, a proper bar, with burgers, wings, beers, and serving wenches, would fit the bill very nicely for me that day. As it so happened, the young lad could fulfill that requirement—apart from the serving wenches—and told me that he'd be happy to drive me into nearby Pawling, where there was a tavern. I enlisted J-Rex and her boyfriend to join me, and we had several beers, wings, and burgers before getting a cab back.

It was the first time I'd spent any time in the company of J-Rex without the Maine Sisters. She came across as a very determined young woman. She was about to relocate to be near Max, who studied on the West Coast. They were a very loving, clear-sighted couple. Like many of my generation, I had formed opinions of younger people without really knowing them. The trail dramatically transformed those opinions, almost uniformly for the better. When you put people together in more than usually difficult situations, you realize that we all bleed the same, fear the same, and we all need other people. The so-called Millennial generation had always appeared feckless and unfocused to me, but hardly any of the younger people I met on the trail were that way inclined.

J-Rex and Max brought that home to me more forcibly than others had to that point. I thought about it later in my tent, concluding that these fearless kids were a terrific celebration of everything that is right in this generation. I couldn't be more proud of them had they been my own.

Despite the fact that my tent was about 20 yards from the railroad line and only 15 yards from the road, I again slept well. There had been several latecomers the previous evening and I met up over breakfast with Bamboo, Ungerwear, Yeti Legs, Naturally Hob, and his wife, Chickadee.

My sluggishness of the previous day seemed to have worn off and, with an early start, a good breakfast, and friendly people, I started out in excellent form. The trail took me through a nature reserve that soon had me reaching for my camera.

I knew I had a long day of about 18 miles ahead of me, hopefully getting to Kent, Connecticut, where my friend Brian was going to meet me and take me back to his home. Despite looking forward to seeing Brian and his wife again, and making a good start, I was soon struggling once more. After about five miles, I knew I was going to have a real problem making it to Kent by 4:30 p.m., our planned time.

I also wanted to spend more time with them, as opposed to turning up as an exhausted shambles, so I called Brian to see if he could pick me up a little earlier, at Schaighticoke Road, near Bulls Bridge. That would allow me to slow my pace and put off what looked to be a veritable roller coaster for the seven miles into Kent the following day. Ever affable, Brian agreed and we met at 2 o'clock on the dot. I was all in at this stage, having only hiked just over 11 miles. During these middle miles, I was aware that I was taking more than my fair share of these shorter days. I could only assume that the fact that I almost never had an intentional zero day meant that I was not fully recovering from the pounding that I was putting my body through.

The evening was great, with Dee cooking roast pork and making much more than would usually be necessary. She expected that I would hoover up most of the leftovers, which, of course, I did. Home cooking is always a joy and I felt very much embraced by my friends. I also had a couple of glasses of wine, the first I had taken since before I'd entered the Smokies in April. Given my early concerns of the feasibility of going three or four days without any booze, I felt I'd comfortably crossed that off my list of issues.

Brian took me back to the trail the following morning, via the business premises that he owned. He showed me around as if I was a VIP, albeit a scruffy one. It was interesting to watch my friend in a different environment to that in which I would normally see him. I was struck by subtle changes in his demeanor. I wondered whether he had had similar feelings about changes within me, though I never asked him. All he had to say was that I was too skinny and it made me look old.

Nice. Only your true friends can insult you that way and remain friends.

Chapter 16: Connecticut

I got back on the trail by 10:30, hoping to get cracking, because I knew that I had a very tough uphill to start the day. A scout troop was hiking ahead of me, so I fell in about 30 yards behind them. Perhaps it might have been smart to have taken note of the ample size and shape of their scout leader. Had I done so, it would have helped me ascertain just how much he knew about hiking and directions, because we continued to march along a flat road when I was sure that we should have been climbing. Eventually, I called ahead to see if he thought we were still on the A.T. He shouted back that we were, pausing momentarily to consult his map as I caught up with his team.

Such unswerving certainty on the part of the chubby scout leader convinced me that he was wrong, so I turned back. I told him that I would whistle with my entirely unused bear-defense system if he needed to turn round. The look in the scout leader's eye told me—completely unequivocally—that I was an idiot.

Retracing my steps, I soon discovered that we had gone at least a quarter of a mile past the turn. I prepared to give them a shrill blast, only to emit an anemic squeak, due to my rusting, untried whistle. I was then forced to shout as loud as I could, "You're going the wrong way," though I have no idea if they ever heard. For all I know, they could still be marching in a straight line, Porky at the helm, ever onward, since I never saw them again.

Despite the fairly late start, and the more undulating terrain, I was able to make camp at the Stewart Hollow Brook Shelter, after 14 miles. The last two or three of those miles were alongside a fast-flowing river on a flat, wide path. I was very pleased with my efforts, and set up camp alongside another vintage hiker, and a new buddy, Lighterknot. We had a friendly chat, during which he tried to get me to understand both how to pronounce his name and to understand what it meant. We retired to our tents, and I fell into a deep sleep, having conquered neither.

Lighterknot was eventually to become my BFF on the trail. I couldn't have chosen a finer man with whom to share the last part of my journey. However, I wouldn't meet him again for another 300 miles, in circumstances that suggested more than a touch of serendipity.

Lighterknot and I set out at about the same time the next morning, although I was only planning to get to a road four miles away. I had arranged to meet Bassman, the section hiker I'd got on so well with a few weeks previously. He had texted me, offering to meet up for breakfast, then run me around to pick up any gear or food that I might need. It was such a thoughtful gesture, and I was looking forward to meeting him again. We arranged to meet at 10 o'clock. I was there on the dot, for he drove up about ten seconds later. My ability to know my own hiking pace was starting to impress even me.

Bassman knew of an excellent diner in West Cornwall, so we went and had our fill of eggs, bacon, home fries, and pancakes. After that, Bassman was as good as his word. He drove me to several places, where I bought food for the next three or four days and a pot in which to cook my rice.

The need for this pot had come about following a disastrous attempt to cook rice directly in my Jet Boil Flash a couple of days before. For some reason totally unknown to me, I had added a single cup of water to my rice instead of the prescribed four cups. I've never been one for diverting from recipe instructions, so I presumed the resulting smell and apparent dryness of the rice a few minutes later was all part of the cooking process. I let the mayhem continue. When young Chip noticed a pungent smell, which could never be attributed to any herb known to man, I realized that I had burned everything. It was a shambles. The cleaning of my pot took about thirty minutes. Basically, this entailed picking small pieces of cruddy, burned rice from the bottom of the pot. I must have also taken away any non-stick properties, because it then became a no-go area for rice or pasta. Boiling water was thus my limit.

Bassman and I wandered round the hardware store, where the only thing I could find was a regular, fairly small saucepan—complete with a tempered-glass lid—so I had to settle for that. As you can imagine, it looked ridiculous, and the pan clanked endlessly on the back of my full pack over the next few weeks.

Bassman dropped me at the trailhead. Before diving back into the forest, I noticed a warning about the difficulty of fording a stream just ahead. A detour, which would have added well over a mile to the hike, was offered. Apparently, the rocks in the stream were not only unstable but also slick, a winning combination. The stream was about 100 yards ahead, so I went to check it out. I concluded, *It can't be that bad*, as if convincing myself, so I decided to go for it.

One of my problems is that, despite regular, strong evidence to the contrary, I think I can do anything, so I pretty much always go for it. It probably won't come as the greatest shock of your life when I tell you that I didn't make it across the stream. I started off well, moving comfortably from rock to rock, until I didn't. I managed to get about ten feet from the other bank, but my tumble into the stream occurred as something of an inevitability. I went down onto both my knees. Part of my pack was under water, though my phone stayed dry. I quickly scrambled out, only to see a small amount of blood trickling down my leg. I wouldn't have worried too much about that, had it not been for the alarming egg-like protuberance that accompanied the blood. After walking for about half a mile, I decided to seek yet another urgent care facility. The swelling was spreading rather expansively, and it looked like I was developing a second knee, about six inches below the original, clambering up to meet its twin.

Alone, in the woods, finding an urgent care facility is a bit tricky, but, as so often, the trail provided. I ran into an A.T. volunteer who was completing some maintenance work on the trail. He told me that he had to finish what he was doing, but, if I would wait at the road a few miles ahead, he would drive me the 20 miles into Torrington, the nearest town of any size.

My new lump was now pushing up against its brother, so my walking slowed drastically. By the time I got to the road, I had just a short wait for my guardian angel.

In Torrington, I reached the clinic about half an hour before it closed. The doctor told me that there wasn't a particular problem, and that the swelling would go down with a night's rest and some icing. The nursing assistant was a hiker. He not only cleaned up the wound, he also arranged a room for me at the Quality Inn. He then ran me down to the hotel in his car. The trail had provided once more.

It had been my nineteenth fall of the trip. Although I wasn't to know it at the time, I still had another 26 to go. Some of these falls would be exponentially more painful, but each one would help mark me forever as an Appalachian Trail thru-hiker.

That night, at the Quality Inn, I spoke with Diane for quite a while on the phone. She was hearing of my third visit to an urgent care facility. I was giving her the normal, probably infuriating, "I'll be fine." Suddenly, she blurted out, "You know what? I am so over this fucking hike." She neither asked me to stop, nor asked me to come home. She just wanted me to know what she was thinking at that stage. After we ended the call, I lay back in my bed and considered her comment.

It had been a tough week, with falls, exhaustion, and friends all in the mix. However, for the first time, I allowed myself the luxury of contemplating the finish. I was certain that I was actually going to make it. The 1,500 mile marker would soon be passed, and I would be on to the last third. At the same time, I realized that I, too, was over it. My thinking had moved from a celebration of the journey to a longing for the destination. I couldn't wait to get there, get it over, then get back home to Diane. Katahdin was drawing me on, but Diane's call had articulated a shift in my thoughts that I hadn't acknowledged to that point.

I was eager to put my leg to the test, so I ordered a cab for 7:30 to make the 20-mile return trip to the trail. I'm not sure if cab companies in rural areas can tell the time or not, yet virtually every one that I used had a very casual acquaintance with the concept of punctuality. They all offered nothing more precise than "He's on his way," a clearly untrue statement in every case. After I'd called twice, a very unenthusiastic guy turned up, determined not to converse with me if he could help it. The silence certainly worked for me, so I leaned back in my seat and dozed.

I had an idea that 20 miles was a possibility for the day. Unfortunately, the early pace was slow, with another Lemon-Squeezer-type affair. The rapidly diminishing rock face made for an uncomfortable, buttock-squeezing five minutes. However, once that was out of the way, I made excellent progress on a well-maintained trail.

My lump, which had subsided considerably, didn't seem to impede my hiking at all. The biggest problem was the overwhelming presence of mosquitoes—or mozzies, as I referred to the unwelcome bastards—that seemed oblivious to the fact that I had covered myself liberally with OFF! spray. They were relentless, and made the day tough. That said, their ubiquitous presence cut down my break time, so I started marking off the miles quite easily. In my regular internal conversations, I tended to allow myself easier targets, often wanting to stop before doing the miles I needed to do. For some reason, that day seemed different, and I stuck with it, eventually getting to the Riga Shelter just before 7 o'clock, with a solid 20 miles tucked away.

There were two young guys at the shelter taking up most of the space. They had been there all day, cheerfully playing the *Catan* board game which, they told me, was the most important item in their packs. They often took zero days in the shelters, playing their game between regular naps. I loved their utter lack of urgency.

The shelter had a magnificent, uninterrupted view to the east, so I set an early alarm call to be able to get a time-lapse video of dawn breaking. Unfortunately, that turned out to be a bit of a non-event. When I woke, two minutes before my alarm was due to go off, I looked out of the tent to be confronted by the valley blanketed in cloud. Later, it started to rain, so I delayed my start while the rain passed through, and had a leisurely breakfast by myself.

Packing everything as quietly as I could, I left my two fellow campers sleeping, and headed out, hoping for another big day. I would be passing the 1,500 mile marker within the first mile, and so was ready for another selfie. Not for the first time I missed whatever was there, and another significant milestone went unrecorded.

Bear Mountain was the first challenge of the day. My guidebook showed clear evidence that the descent would turn out to be the toughest part. It was so steep, with the earlier rain making the rocks dangerously slippery. I started to get anxious climbing up—with good reason. While the climb itself was fairly taxing, the top of the descent was as bad as I'd been led to believe. I was ultra-cautious and took about 45 minutes to cover a very short distance, using small footholds and handholds all the way, not slipping once. Then, when I was back on the flat, I skidded and fell for the twentieth time. *Plus ça change...*

Chapter 17: Massachusetts

I was now making my way through Sage's Ravine, my first real landmark in a new state, Massachusetts. Sage's Ravine was a bewitching trail that followed the river deep in the ravine, with dark greens interspersed with the sunshine protruding from above. The whole scene was plunged into darkness and light the whole way through. It would have been a terrific picture day, but I wasn't able to oblige because my battery was dying.

The day was especially bad for steep climbs followed by rocky descents, while the spectacular cliff-top views from Race Mountain were my favorites. Mount Everett was a lung-bursting ascent, followed by another seat-of-my-pants descent—in this case literally and deliberately—that made me take my time. The Virginia ridges were now a remote memory and these taxing miles in the southern part of New England were preparing me for the White Mountains and Maine.

Eventually, I'd done my mileage target, so I took the opportunity to visit the Appalachian Trail Conservancy's Kellogg Conservation Center, just off the trail at Mass41. For some reason I seemed to think that this would be a place at which I could tent, though nobody appeared to be about. Taking absence as acquiescence, I walked into a room at the back, finding a power outlet to charge my phone. Eventually, I bumped into a guy who worked on the property, though not for A.T.C. He told me that I shouldn't be there, so I packed up and moved on. I had clearly misinterpreted what the place was all about.

It was now getting close to 5 o'clock, and I was scrambling to find somewhere to stay. I certainly didn't fancy a night by the side of the road in this desolate area. I called a number in my *Thru-hikers Companion* for Jess Treat, who lets out two bedrooms in her home. The downside was that I had to hike another three or four miles. Fortunately, I got to US7 in about 90 minutes, thanks to a stretch of fairly flat terrain.

Jess was away, but her friend, the slightly whimsical but absolutely charming Heath, proved to be a great substitute. She picked me up at the roadside, then offered me a beer as I walked in. Jess was only charging $35, plus $5 for laundry. For that, I got a clean, comfortable bed in my own room, a lovely shower, breakfast, and shuttles to and from the trail. This was a bargain that I would highly recommend.

Heath served up a great breakfast of blueberry pancakes the next morning, then took me and Slow, an older guy from Ocala, in Florida, back to the trailhead. Slow was recovering from an injury and certainly lived up to his name. He moved almost glacially, so much so that he looked as if he was going backwards. We separated within seconds and I plunged into the woods.

The terrain was far easier than the day before, with both the ups and the downs much less intense. I maintained my regular two miles an hour for several hours, passing through the odd meadow, but mainly under the green tunnel. Some climbs were prolonged, for the day was basically up and over East Mountain, then up and over Mount Wilcox. As a consequence, I took several breaks and my rate started to slow.

I was tempted at one point to hang out for a couple of hours at Benedict Pond, which had a side trail leading to a beach. However, I was still over 30 miles ahead of my self-imposed schedule. I was aware that New Hampshire and Maine would claw back some of that surplus, so I didn't want to slack off now that I was ahead of the game.

There was another, unmarked, though equally glorious pond at nearly 2,000 feet, near the top of Mount Wilcox. I took the opportunity to add to my growing list of pictures posted to Facebook. While I know that some hikers sneered at the growing incursion of technology into the wilderness, I could think of nothing better than sharing these beautiful moments with friends and the people I loved. For many, these pictures enabled them to vicariously hike with me. Some of the folks in my in-laws' assisted living facility also followed the hike. Diane would show them all my posts and photos regularly, while some of them followed my blog. How can anybody deny that sort of access to people whose only form of exercise is going to the bathroom several times a day?

After an 18-mile day, spent mainly at 1,500-2,000 feet, I descended deep into the woods to reach Shaker Campsite, where I met a couple of local guys out for a week's hiking with their sons. The site had tenting platforms, which were becoming more common the further north I headed. These platforms allowed me to use my poles to set up my tent—as opposed to spikes—and guaranteed a flat sleeping position, a conundrum that I had continued to be unable to solve on any regular basis, even after all these miles.

As often happened, the guys were intrigued by my thru-hike, and we chatted as we prepared and ate dinner. The unrelenting onslaught from the mozzies eventually drove us into our respective tents, where we remained for the rest of the night.

The following morning, I took a brief hike into Tyringham, which was just a short way off the trail. At the post office, there was a food package from Diane, so I consolidated my pack. These resupply stops always reminded me of the weight of food I had to carry, a fact that became instantly apparent once the pack was hoisted back over my shoulders.

The huffing and puffing that followed were entirely consistent with the increased weight. That difference never failed to surprise me, but, once I settled down, the pack seemed to become part of me, and I moved on.

I had decided that the mozzies were just too bad to put up with, so I incorporated a trip into Lee, the next town. There, I would buy a face net to at least keep the darn things at bay. Luckily, a friendly old lady—who must have been at least 85—stopped to my outstretched thumb, offering me a lift into Lee. She was an extraordinarily vibrant woman, often referring to "older people" unselfconsciously, and fully engaged in the number of miles I had hiked to this point. She took me directly to the hardware store, where she insisted that they would have what I needed. With a smile and a wave, she zoomed away.

A face net, a large canister of OFF!, and a smaller, more devastating bottle of bug spray, completed my shopping. I headed across the road to a local breakfast joint to demolish the "Hiker's Special," a plate of everything you might consider having for breakfast, along with several things that you wouldn't. Naturally, I hoovered it all down with gusto, charged my phone, then caught a cab back to the trailhead.

It was now past noon, so I altered my target to get to the Upper Goose Pond Cabin, making it just an 11-mile day. The cabin was run by the A.T.C. and had caretakers, tent sites, the cabin itself, the undeniable luxury of two privies, and, most invitingly, a large pond in which to swim. They also provided pancakes for breakfast. I only discovered this the following morning, after I'd eaten my oatmeal, protein powder, and fruit concoction. Undeterred, I still stuffed down six pancakes slathered with butter and syrup. Of course I did.

When I had reached the cabin the previous evening, I wandered round to take it all in, then enjoyed a languid swim in the pond. Even without soap, it felt like one of the finest, most exhilarating showers of my life. With a few other hikers around, it had all the charm of a smelly man's spa.

On the way to the cabin, I ran into the guys I had camped with the night before. One, who bore a striking resemblance to Bradley Cooper, was heading back to the road. He told me that his friend had blown out his knee and was leaving the trail. I thought that this was a great shame, as they had all clearly been having a blast. "Bradley Cooper" was taking the boys on to complete their hike, but this sudden issue reminded me how lucky I'd been to have remained fairly well unscathed on my hike thus far. All hikers were aware that one false step could end their adventure in an instant. As we got closer to Katahdin, we faced that possibility with growing anxiety, hoping that we wouldn't be the one who had to go home in this way.

That night, with no real prospect of rain in the forecast, it surprised nobody that it poured mightily. With the rain dancing merrily off the tenting platform, I stayed dry and warm in my tent, content to have found this great spot, still living my dream.

Over pancakes the next day, I was joined at the table by Smiles and Critter, two southbound hikers, as well as Triple P and her fellow hiker, Chicka Chee. Triple P stood for Purple Polish Pimp. She was trying, for reasons best known to herself, to tag fellow hikers by asking if they would let her put purple nail polish on at least one fingernail.

Now this would normally be a ridiculous proposition to most people. In the forest, on that morning, it felt the most reasonable request in the world. Smiles and Critter each had one nail tagged, so I held out my left hand and had Triple P mark the index and middle finger. For Brits, holding up these two fingers with the nails towards your face means victory. It was a much-loved salute favored by Winston Churchill in the Second World War. Holding the nails outwards, for a Brit, is rather more vulgar. I contented myself with my very British response to her request.

I should also say that I had no idea quite how long polish stays on the nail. There were still remnants of it two or three weeks later. To be fair, this may have had something to do with the infrequency of my washing. Triple P certainly left her mark on me, and my fellow hikers, for some time.

As I was leaving camp, "Bradley Cooper" called me over and offered me his friend's head net, which was excellent for vision and certainly better than the one I had bought. I gratefully accepted. I soon paid it forward, as I met up soon after with Green Lantern, another southbounder, giving him my spare net with a warning of imminent mozzie attacks.

I was going for an 18-mile day, though I also wanted to pop in to see the famous Cookie Lady, where I intended to charge my phone and fill up on as many cookies as possible.

Massachusetts will always be the muddy, wet, and mozzie state for me. The hiking would have been terrific had it been dry, but it became a mucky mess. It was really tricky to negotiate some of the quagmires that I encountered. That said, I made good progress that day, passing the beautiful Finnerty Pond. These high-elevation ponds had an other-worldly feel about them. They became my favorite feature of the North, in the same way that balds had been my favorite in the South. My brother Mike reminded me that I was in James Fenimore Cooper country. I could look across those ponds and, in the silence of the woods, it was thrilling to imagine Hawkeye and Chingachgook paddling towards me in their canoe. Of course, had that actually happened I would have crapped myself at the sight.

The Cookie Lady lived about 150 yards from the trail. I took this detour, only to see that her stall was closed and the place looked deserted. I was just about to venture nearer to the house—in the hope that there was an outside power point—when she swung her car into the drive, taking it directly into her garage. Encouraged, I walked towards her house, only to see her disappear indoors, leaving me feeling somewhat at a loss as to what I should do. I needn't have worried, for she returned a few moments later with a couple of blueberry cookies in a basket. She sold lemonade and Coke, so I bought a couple of cans of the former and asked if I could plug in my phone to charge. She didn't appear to understand the concept, so I had to point at the vacant power point at the side of her garage. She vaguely waved her acceptance.

By now I was thinking of staying, as the Cookie Lady allowed hikers to tent in her field. However, the cookies had given me a bit of a sugar rush, so I chose instead to move on and make the next shelter, Kay Wood Shelter, in order to keep stacking up the miles. After a while, I caught up with Triple P. She was trying to get all the way to Dalton, a few miles past the shelter, so we hiked together until we went our separate ways.

The sun dropping in the sky always had a beautiful effect on the forest, bathing it with a distinct, dark greenness as the light created growing shadows through the trees.

There was a group of young high school volunteers, along with their group leaders, at the shelter, as well as a female section hiker. The volunteers were doing trail repairs, so the section hiker and I spoke at length with them about the work they were doing. Once more, my preconceived ideas about the younger generation were called into question. My judgmental gene was getting a real workout on this trip and has rarely resurfaced since I returned. For that alone, I am grateful.

Chapter 18: The mountains start again

The absolutely worst time of day for rain was in the couple of hours before waking. A two-hour drenching gives you no opportunity to pack up dry, and I was treated to this the following morning. After breakfast, I sulkily packed my wet tent, then headed into Dalton to try and get a second breakfast. The extra weight alone was irritating enough, while the dampness creeping into my underwear was an added bonus I could have done without.

I reached the town in about an hour. Following the white blazes down a street, I heard "Mighty Blue," shouted from a porch. The house was owned by a hiker-friendly guy who—

quite bravely in my view—allowed hikers to tent on his lawn and his porch. In residence were Spider, Yeti Legs, and Tumbles, as well as several others whose names I couldn't recall. Yeti Legs—of the grey underpants—had bought a black pair, which at least had the effect of revealing a little less. He had also bought a shirt, so he was substantially overdressed.

Tumbles was providing haircuts for all who wanted them. At the time, he was shaving Spider's head and exposing why Spider was so-called: his dome sported a complete tattoo of a spider's web. His hair fell away and the web gradually materialized.

I noticed that most of the guys also had one or several purple fingers, so I knew where Triple P had stayed the previous night. Tumbles willingly gave me a trim, and I left in search of breakfast. Jacob's Pub promised to be hiker-friendly. Indeed, it turned out to be so. The manager allowed me to come in and charge my phone, while the staff cleaned up around me before opening. A grilled Reuben sandwich and two Yuenglings slowed down my resolve to leave. However, I knew that I needed to get moving. I was hoping to reach Cheshire and stay at the Harbour House Inn.

The trip was blighted due to constant thunder and lightning, even though only sprinkles of rain fell. I was making good headway when the storm finally decided that it had had enough of playing around with me and gave me a good dousing. On top of that, it chose to pelt me with hail that seemed to grow larger the harder it rained. To be frank, I was a bit nonplussed as to what to do. The only shelter appeared to be trees.

Unsurprisingly, this made absolutely no difference to the hail, and I was getting perilously colder and wetter by the second.

As I stood there, starting to feel the chill and dampness engulf me from the neck down, I felt more exposed than at any time on the trail. I'd comfortably dealt with animals, I'd become very used to sleeping in my tent with nobody around, and I'd even hardened my limbs to cope with the rigors thrown at me. But this was a dilemma for which I had no rational answer. My shortcomings as a hiker were coming home to roost.

In the end, I chose simply to keep hiking. I figured that at least I'd warm up, and so it proved. Unfortunately, I was in such a hurry to get down the mountain—shocked at how blindsided I had been by the hail—that I made a wrong turn about a mile from the bottom. I had been striding purposefully, but hadn't seen a white blaze for a while. I became increasingly worried that I'd gone the wrong way when I suddenly arrived at a road. Frankly, I was relieved to be there.

The rain had stopped. I was cold and soaked through. I got my phone and checked Google Maps to establish where I was. I discovered that I was about a mile from where I should have been. I called Eva, the owner at the Harbour House Inn and told her where Google Maps was placing me. Sadly for me, my wrong turn had not only taken me off the trail, it had also taken me down the wrong side of the mountain. Eva suggested that I might go back into the forest, then try to find the right route, calling her again when I was back on track. I looked at the phone, trying to transmit my incredulity to her. It didn't work. As I had suspected, this turned out to be a laughable suggestion for somebody with my navigational abilities. I was soon even more lost, yet somehow bushwhacked my way back to my previously incorrect spot. On this occasion, Eva must have taken pity on my whining and came to find me. My mini drama was over.

An hour later, I had showered, my clothes were in the washer, and I was sitting in a beautiful living room, drinking tea and munching cookies. I still had to find my way back up the mountain and back on track, yet, for the time being, I was glad to be safe. I was also learning that being warm and dry indoors is a privilege, not a right, and one I vowed never to take for granted again. Despite a few other broken promises to myself, I never have.

Having made such a complete cock-up of my exit from the mountain, I was faced with a daunting prospect the following morning. Eva was dropping me back at the spot where I should have emerged from the woods the previous day, not where I did emerge.

Her terrific breakfast helped keep my fear of early-morning orienteering at bay, and confirmed to me that this was one of my favorite stops on the trail. The place was so hiker-friendly that she charged hikers half her normal rate. While $85 isn't cheap in the normal run of things on the A.T., it was a bargain as far as I was concerned. It revitalized me after my lost-in-the-mountains odyssey.

I couldn't put off the restart forever, so I was eventually left to trace the A.T. back up the mountain. On the way, I ran into a southbound hiker called Three by Five. He was also lost. I felt infinitely better that I wasn't the only idiot loose in the forest. I eventually found the spot where I went wrong, tapped the white blaze with my pole, then hiked back down to start my day. I waved at Three by Five as I passed him. He looked at me as if I was crazy.

I had been hiking for about an hour when I turned over my arm to check for bugs or, more particularly, for ticks. Neither was there, though the previously down-facing side of my right forearm was completely covered in blood. There is nothing like an armful of blood to grab your attention. I stopped to see where it was coming from. There was a sterile gauze pad in my medical kit, so I used that to clean the arm thoroughly. I was unable to see either a recent cut or even a re-opened old wound. The only assumption that I could make was that I must have knocked off a scab from a tiny previous cut and it must have bled profusely, then stopped.

Odd to me as that was, later in the day at the Wilbur Clearing Shelter, I was chatting with a couple of female section hikers and a southbound guy. We all then retired to our tents. I discovered when wiping my face with a baby wipe—my only cleaning system on the trail—that I had dried, crusted blood on the left side of my nose. Nobody had mentioned it and, with no mirrors, I had no idea that it was there. When I cleared that blood off, I took a dark selfie to discover a small nick on my nose. I had bled many times before—and I certainly did later—but these two events came within hours of one another, with neither warning nor obvious cause. Spooky.

It had already been a significant day for northbounders. We had gone above 3,000 feet for the first time since Shenandoah National Park—some 600 miles back—with the magnificent Mount Greylock as our highest point. There was a fair amount of uphill trudging on my part, so I took my time and trudged away.

I eventually made it, and was rewarded by the fact that there was a lodge at the top, serving soft drinks, several of which I downed gratefully. I also took the opportunity to recharge my phone, dozing on a bench while I did so. A child pointed me out to his father, asking him, "Is that man alright?" While I couldn't precisely attest to the answer to that question, I stuck my hand in the air. The wave appeared to reassure him that I was, at the very least, still alive.

There was still a three-mile descent to Wilbur Clearing Shelter, so I set off reluctantly from my somnolent position. My movement was apparently much to the relief of my inquiring young friend. I reached my goal just before dark, in good time for dinner. It had been a 13-mile day, so just a shade under my target. Given that I'd gone over Mount Greylock, I was pleased with my effort. Tenting just behind the shelter, I cleaned that mysterious blood from my face before falling asleep.

I set my alarm for 5:15 on the Saturday morning, intending to do the three or so miles into North Adams, in time for a second breakfast of the day. I was hoping to charge my phone and link up to Wi-Fi. My soccer team, the real Mighty

Blues, was playing its first game of a new season, and I wanted to listen to the commentary.

It could not have worked out better. I got into town, consulted Yelp on my iPhone to establish a decent nearby breakfast joint, then pitched up to Renee's Diner. Once online, I ordered the Super Hungry Man breakfast, for which I felt supremely qualified. A plate full of eggs, bacon, corned beef hash, French toast and syrup, several coffees, plus a toasted blueberry muffin, and a victory for my team, left me a contented man. I waddled from the diner after a thoroughly enjoyable detour of nearly three hours. My blowout required finding somewhere to stay for the night. The nearest shelter was too close, while the next one was too far. If nothing else, I needed to walk off some of the three or four thousand calories sloshing around in my stomach.

On the way, I moved into Vermont—my twelfth state—at Mile 1,593. There were more extensive climbs, and, by about 6 o'clock, I came across a father and his two young kids camping out for the weekend. They had found a tiny clearing behind some reeds, by a dried-out pond. We were at Roaring Branch, and it seemed to fit the bill for me. I spent a relaxed evening chatting with him while I prepared and ate a bowl of pasta. I'd had another day a shade under my mileage target, but, given the earlier detour, not a bad effort at all.

My fellow tenter mentioned that the previous evening, when he had been camping in the same spot, he was sure that a bear had passed through the camp. Despite this worrying report he seemed sanguine about hanging his food in a tree. It was certainly my normal practice, so I hung my two food bags and went to bed. Sure enough, at about 2 o'clock that night, I heard an animal moving about outside. I didn't think it was a bear, because it didn't make much noise: more sniffing than tramping about. I thought it may have been the guy getting up to relieve himself but, when I asked him in the morning, he had thought it was me for the same reason.

Nothing happened, though it affirmed my practice of placing my food outside of my tent. I did this just in case an animal should decide to come and join me in search of food. I don't care how brave you are: a 400-pound hungry bear wouldn't be your first choice for a nocturnal visitor.

My neighbors had got on the trail early, leaving me to quietly enjoy my breakfast in the silence of the woods. I had only the waking birds as occasional company, while the sun gradually—and lavishly—lit up the day. Those quiet moments, always impossible to capture in either video or photo, remain the most wonderful memories of breaking dawn on the trail.

My mission to watch the last day of each of the major golf championships depended upon getting in front of a TV for the U.S. P.G.A. Championship. I was already on the case. The three days leading up to each of the tournament finishes involved planning where I was going to be ahead of time. This was going to be no exception; in fact, my almost three hour calorie-fest the previous day was all part of my plan to get to VT9 by lunchtime on that Sunday.

Another rocky, mucky hike of eight or nine miles got me there right on time, following a hair-raising descent down to the road in the last half-mile. These tiring downs were stressing my knees. A combination of rocks and tree roots caused havoc, with potential catastrophe at every step. Fortunately, I was able to negotiate the path, and called a shuttle. I was taken to another mediocre motel which, at least, had working Wi-Fi and a laundry facility.

It's also worth pointing out that I passed the 1,600-mile mark soon after leaving my glorious spot at Roaring Branch. I regarded this achievement as awesome in itself, yet, with the end less than 600 miles away, only finishing on Katahdin would do for me now. That brought Katahdin and eventual success more into focus. However, I tried to play it down in my mind because those 600 miles were going to be as tough as any on the trail. For some of my fellow hikers, the journey remained what it was all about. While the journey was also important to me, the destination had now taken on greater significance in my thoughts. I would only be satisfied if I could have that picture, at the top of that mountain, forever in my possession.

With a rain delay in the golf, I was able to shower, do my laundry, and get to the micro-brewery pub before the leaders teed off. I set myself up at the corner of the bar, with a perfect view of the TV, then ate like a man condemned to death. As a bit of a bonus, the Irishman Rory McIlroy won his second consecutive major championship. I was able to reflect upon a weekend of self-indulgent sports, both watching and listening.

I'd really enjoyed my time, but I knew that there were no more golf stops for me.

Back in my room, I set myself the target of returning to a 100-mile week in order to pass 1,700 miles by the following Sunday. It was going to be difficult—with the increasing height and severity of the mountains ahead—but I'd grown confident in my ability to do this. All I needed was the luck to back up that confidence. Although, with many falls still to come, I certainly pushed that luck to the limit.

Chapter 19: Vermont

Monday was a very quiet day, with hardly any extended contact with other hikers. More and more southbounders—known as SOBOs—were passing through, with warnings and praise in equal measure for New Hampshire and Maine. The expression I'd heard that tended to intimidate NOBOs—most especially me—went along the following lines. When a NOBO has done 80 percent of the miles, he has only expended 20 percent of the effort. If this was in any respect true, then I was probably, well, fucked. There was absolutely no possibility that I could expend four times the amount of effort I had already left out on the trail, let alone the 60 pounds in weight. I tried to treat these expressions with disdain, although this one seemed to be about to hit me squarely in the face. I would always be cheered by positive stories from SOBOs, while I studiously avoided thinking too much about the negative ones.

There was quite a bit of climbing on this day, with the 3,748-foot Glastenbury Mountain the highlight. I met a funny old woman at the top who was all doom and gloom about pretty much everything. She told me that it was going to pour with rain before I reached the next shelter, which it didn't. It was going to pour with rain all night, which it also didn't. Lastly, she shared with me that "hundreds of people" get killed in the White Mountains every year in August. Once again, utter nonsense.

Leaving old Misery Guts as quickly as possible, I headed down to Kid Gore Shelter, where I had planned to tent, though the official tent site was 50 yards farther on. Checking that out, I ran into an older guy, who was section hiking with his dog. There were no good spots other than the one he had tented on, so I set up camp back at the shelter and started to prepare dinner. The old guy came to visit with his dog and a flask of scotch. "For cocktails," he declared. I declined, as I really don't like scotch, but we had a few laughs. We were eventually joined by two young hikers—Chip, who I had been seeing regularly for some time, and Denali, who I hadn't seen for several hundred miles. I recalled that Denali had previously worn a long bird feather in his hair and, amazingly, it was still there.

Despite the crazy old woman's prediction, it didn't rain in the night, so I was able to pack up nice and dry. I set off early, expecting to get at least 15 miles in, though hoping for 20. The previous two days had been quite tough, with the miles harder to complete. I couldn't explain it, other than to say that I'd gotten tired, and was worrying a little about hitting the tougher mountains further north. My weight had dipped even more, and I may have been losing a bit of strength. All the same, you tend to notice these things when you're out in the woods for several hours at a time, and they gain traction in your mind.

It was another day of trudging through a very dense forest, with few, if any, incidents or views. The big push of the day was up and over Stratton Mountain, at nearly 4,000 feet. I spoke with Diane prior to this climb and must have sounded a bit fed up. I had stopped for lunch. Having slipped a few times that morning, I felt that the climb was going to exhaust any remaining strength that I had. As soon as I'd finished speaking with Diane, I realized that I'd selfishly pushed my worries onto her, so I gave myself a proverbial kick up the backside. As always on the A.T., there was no alternative but to go forward.

I spooned about a third of a jar of peanut butter down my gullet, along with a wrap containing mayo, sun-dried tomatoes, and tuna. I was instantly energized, and got stuck into the climb, making the top at a good pace. Rain was clearly closing in, so I revised my target for the day to Stratton Pond Shelter, just over three miles down the mountain. I was really moving on the way down, but had to remain aware of my propensity to fall when hurrying. I eventually got to Stratton Pond Shelter in just over an hour, with the rain holding off, and no more falls to record. It was only about 3:30 p.m. by now, but I decided that my luck was holding, so I called it a day.

Luckily, a friendly group of people accumulated in the shelter that evening. Already there were Mike and Emily, a young couple section hiking in the early stages of their relationship. I can't imagine how that conversation must have gone when he asked her out on a date, though it seemed to be working out well. If you can bond with a woman when both of you have the faint odor of a couple of discarded dog turds, then you must have a chance when you return to the land of hot showers and flush toilets. Later, we were joined by a pair of savvy young female hikers, who were out for a few days, then Yeti Legs, Tumbles and, a little later, Breaktime. We had one of those evenings that make the trail so social, eventually settling down in the shelter to see out the impending storm.

Before that, Mike and I each took a couple of bottles and went to get water from the advertised spring, trying to follow directions from the two young girls. Without wishing to stereotype us, we soon ignored the girls' instructions, and, as men often do, we got lost. We were utterly unable to find the stream, ultimately filling our bottles from Stratton Pond. This was an error, for the pond water smelled suspiciously like sweat. It was also appropriately warm, though we only discovered this on returning to the shelter. Giving more thought to it, many sweaty hikers must have swum in that very spot, so we restricted use of the water to cooking. There was certainly an added saltiness to my pasta that had previously been missing. However,

I was less able to enjoy it, given my suspicions. I'd like to say that this resulted in a new attitude on my part about women giving directions, but I can't say that it has.

It rained intermittently during the night, so we all knew that there was more rain due the next day. The calculation consequently became when to leave and where to head for. My inclination was that there was no point in expecting the weather to get much better, so leaving straight after breakfast seemed the only way forward. I decided to go for Manchester Center, about ten miles away. My hope was that I could get into town, stock up on a few things, then get out if the weather was okay. If this went as planned, I'd end up in a shelter a few miles further down the trail.

The wind was very powerful, piercing through the trees and blowing the earlier rain off the leaves, making it look as if it was raining. As the miles passed, however, the wind got wilder and the rain started to fall, moderately at first, then a little stronger. I was only about three miles from the road into town when it started to really come down. Luckily, there was a shelter five minutes ahead of me. I made it just before the clouds opened up. Yeti Legs and Tumbles joined me 15 minutes later, wet, but happy for the respite. The third member of their group, Breaktime, had obviously ignored the shelter, continuing to the road. After about an hour, the two guys put on their waterproofs, then braved the pouring rain and high winds to try and catch up with him. I stayed to see if things would ease off.

With the rain battering my shelter, I was entertained for a while by a crazy mouse careening around the building in constant laps. He started by the entrance, climbed up onto the table, rushed past my food bag—with a sly glance—hopped off onto a beam, then finally leaped down to the floor, before reaching the entrance once more, and beginning the process again. He was mesmerizing.

After about half an hour of this riveting entertainment, I took the plunge and made my way carefully, but fairly quickly, down the mountain. I had managed to locate a place to stay, so I headed off in high hopes of having a shower, generally cleaning up, and getting a bite to eat.

Unfortunately, my phone didn't have a signal at the road, so I was unable to call the motel once I got there. So, there I was again, with my thumb in the air with some urgency. I figured my chances of getting a lift were decreasing with every additional raindrop that fell on me. At the best of times, and in the best of weather, I was hardly the type you'd like to see on your leather seats. I was now starting to leak from every possible orifice. A lovely old French couple took pity on me, screeched to a halt, and delivered me to the Red Sled Motel.

The motel was run by an Englishman, John, who had been in the States for 50 years, though his British accent remained strong. His was so distinctively from the north west of England that I remarked upon it. We reminisced about England as if it existed in another time and place. For the two of us, it probably did. John gave me a hiker rate of $70 and offered to do my laundry for another $7. The room was clean, though a little dated, but he also provided Netflix, which was a welcome first for me on the trail. For only another $5, he ran me a couple of miles to the outfitter in town, then returned to collect me from the excellent Firefly Bar and Grill a few hours later. The juxtaposition of the words "bar" and "grill" always attracted me on this trip. The combination rarely disappointed.

John returned me to the trail, and I was back at it by 8 o'clock the following morning. The rain was now forgotten and the sun started its climb in the sky.

Bromley Mountain was the first peak of the day. I started off like a train, devouring the three miles to the top in just over 75 minutes. I was going so well that, on the way up, I followed a sign that promised a vista, where I sat on a rock for a snack. I gazed down at further evidence, as if more were needed, of the beauty of America, from south to north. Before I'd started the hike I knew that I would see an elevated view of dramatic scenery. But I was completely unprepared for the range and consistent beauty that passed in front of me every single day. It takes effort to get there, but I can assure anybody who might be tempted that you won't be disappointed once you've made the effort.

Bromley Mountain was a ski mountain. The last 400 or so yards were through a meadow that was doubtless an easy, wide ski run. For me, it was just another uphill slog. At the top, the wind was blowing wildly, so I ducked behind a hut and caught the sun out of the wind for 20 minutes before moving on. Somewhat incongruously, there was what must have once been regarded as a futuristic-looking ski gondola which looked as if it had been lifted straight from the *Jetsons*. The descent was initially very steep and rocky—rarely a favorite combination—but I managed to negotiate it without too many issues.

I sat having lunch a while later at the top of Peru Peak. The climb included a lot of very tricky rocks to negotiate on the way up, and I started to think ahead again. For once, it wasn't Katahdin that I was thinking of. I was more focused on the upcoming topography in my guide. Things were about to get real and, when that happened, I would almost certainly fall. That was something to look forward to.

I reached Big Branch Shelter at 5 o'clock. It looked like I was going to have a quiet night to myself, when Chip and some friends turned up. Chip, I had noticed, carried a guitar with him at all times, and I realized that I had never seen him play it. When I mentioned this peculiarity to him, he looked as if it hadn't occurred to him before. He confirmed that, in the entire trip to this point, he hadn't plucked a single note.

Along with Chip, there was a young woman, Stardust—of whom more later—as well as the appropriately named Viking, who looked very much like one of that breed. He turned out, however, to be extremely articulate and knowledgeable about the whole camping experience. Not for the first time, and certainly not for the last, the words "book" and "cover" sprang to mind.

We all sat around together, preparing our respective dinners, while Viking set a fire. The ever-adventurous Chip decided to set up his hammock between two trees that put part of the hammock directly over the rushing, and very loud, river. The river was our water source. Just retrieving water from it was a noisy, chaotic experience. Quite how anybody could sleep with the torrent cascading four or five feet below him all night long was simply beyond me. As always, Chip was up for it.

I turned in and left my friends around the camp fire. A few minutes later I smiled quietly to myself in my tent, as Chip started strumming away to break his 1,600-mile guitar abstinence on the trail. It was well worth the wait.

My Appalachian Trial II: Creaking Geezer, Hidden Flagon

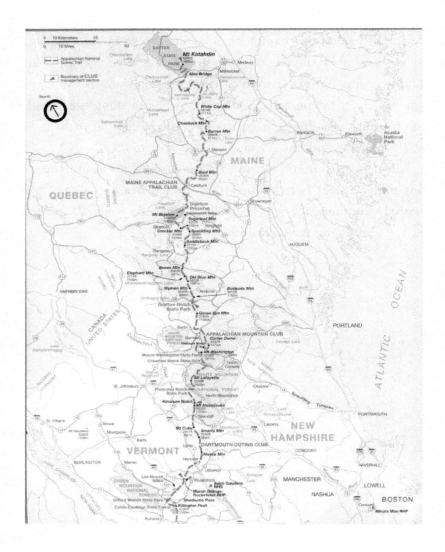

Chapter 20: Killington and beyond

A very chilly night left me thankful that my woolen hat was going to be with my mail drop in Danby. The road into town was only about a mile from the shelter, so I set out hoping to cadge a lift from a passing car. Emerging from the trees, I realized that a ride was unlikely. I was on a mountain road that led up to the top, but nowhere beyond. It didn't faze me too much, because my guidebook had indicated that it was just over one mile into Danby. However, I checked Google Maps, only to discover that Danby was actually four miles away. I was not happy.

With no other option, I started walking. I eventually passed a small community of houses, where I was joined by a boxer dog, rather worryingly named Chomper. I heard a neighbor call him a few times, but he seemed eager to follow me, ignoring any attempts to halt his adventure by my side. Perhaps it was my over-developed odor that drew him to me. I started to get worried about Chomper as we approached an intersection with a main road. He was a little free-spirited in nature, and seemed oblivious to anything I would say to him. Quite why I thought that a dog might understand me, I can't explain—even my wife often has trouble. Nonetheless, I was constantly talking to him, warning him to be careful.

At the intersection, I ran into young Stardust, from the previous evening. She had been lucky enough to get a lift behind me. A woman had stopped for her but refused to stop for me. Apparently, I was guilty of the heinous crime of being a man. Stardust and I checked Chomper's collar and found the number of a veterinarian. When we called, the vet asked us take Chomper to the nearby gas station, where he would come and collect him. Stardust took him there, leaving me to cross the busy road without a potential dead dog on my conscience.

I got my package and went to Nichols Country Store for coffee, a donut, two eggs, cheese and bacon sandwiches, plus two slices of French toast, butter, syrup, and bacon. The owner was clearly used to hikers clogging their arteries in this manner. She asked one of her customers if he minded dropping me back to the trail. He agreed, even though it was clearly out of his way to the tune of about eight miles. He was a terrific guy and another dollop of Trail Magic was much appreciated.

Back on the trail, I was going well until I must have taken another wrong turn down the mountain. I was lost once more. Shaking my head and berating myself, I trudged back uphill, but was unable to find the trail for another 40 minutes. I eventually got moving again, covering nearly four miles in 90 minutes before reaching Minerva Hinchey Shelter.

I was feeling sorry for myself at this point. I had wasted the four miles earlier in the day, as well as several more miles by getting lost. My rational self redressed the balance by pointing out that I had still done my 13 miles. Having that imaginary target every day helped me keep my focus on the goal. That night, even though I was particularly ticked with myself, the fact that I'd achieved my target balanced the scales considerably.

I slept a lot better than I had recently, and woke ready to get up and over Mount Killington. My loneliness motivated me more each day. I wanted to move on in order to finish and return home. I was hoping to enjoy New Hampshire and Maine, though I suspected they would become a grind. All I could do was continue with my plan, and I'd be able to get there in time to return home for Diane's birthday at the end of September.

I had another day that was marked by a lack of energy almost from the start, feeding myself relentlessly, but to no avail. My immediate goal was Cooper Lodge at the top of Killington, which would maintain my target mileage. However, I stopped so many times during the climb that I began to doubt I would achieve even that. The path ahead looked intimidating, while the darkness in the woods exacerbated the intimidation. With stops at the two intervening shelters—including a 20-minute nap at the second one—I eventually got there after about nine hours on the trail. I was exhausted and felt very low.

There was a good crowd developing, but I wasn't in the mood to mingle. I had a quick dinner of rice, managing to burn the bottom of my pot in the process, then set up my tent and climbed in. Of course, it poured through the night to put the icing on my day. Sometimes, the relentless struggle would just wear me down. My only response was to write it off, in the hope that things would improve the next morning. This philosophy got me through several bad moments, though in this case, the improvement wasn't immediate.

Unfortunately, I had forgotten to fasten one clip in my tent, and there was a pool of water at one end when I woke. My pack was soaked, so I decided that I would get into town and book a room as soon as possible. My irritation was near to breaking point. I needed to get off the trail for the night. When other people piss you off, you can always walk away. When you piss yourself off, you're keeping bad company, from which there is no escape.

Latecomers had tented next to me, including Hobo Nobo and Caddyshack, the positive, very friendly middle-aged women I had last seen about 200 miles back. "Great," I muttered to myself, "I'm hiking at the pace of a middle-aged woman. Bloody marvelous." This, from a man in his 60s, was considerably less than reasonable, though reason had flown out the window by this stage. I allowed myself the luxury of bitching and moaning to my heart's content. I can't say that it helped a lot, but it certainly allowed me the opportunity to unleash a few well-chosen words at myself and, for that, I felt better.

Sometimes, you have to take what you can from the day.

The walk down the mountain was easier than the previous day's uphill, though it was often precipitous. With the rocks and roots dramatically affected by the previous night's rain, it was slow going.

I booked into the Inn at Long Trail, an absolute bargain at $58, including Wi-Fi, laundry, and a full breakfast. The fact that there was an Irish pub downstairs did nothing to harm the inn's credentials as far as I was concerned. I took lavish advantage of this gem.

It had been a miserable couple of days for me, and I even entertained the thought that I might quit. Had the inn not been so hospitable, I may well have thrown in the towel that night. Old habits kicked in, as if by magic. I brightened up, lunched, then later dinnered, and drank a few pints of beer. After all, despite my lousy mood, I had still completed eight miles from the top of Killington. I was aware that I could stop at any moment and return home, but I was driven on more than ever by my fierce desire to have that celebratory picture on the top of Katahdin. After all, there was less than 500 miles to go. Almost a walk in the park.

I had to hike for about half a mile to get back to the A.T. the following morning. I knew that I'd be crossing the 1,700-mile barrier within a mile or so, though physical markers had been missing for the previous 400 miles. Of course, this time, there were two markers about 200 yards apart. I snapped pictures of both for posterity.

The magnificent Kent Pond was my companion for about 30 minutes early on this day. The trail curled around it, affording me some dazzling shots of what I would refer to as a lake. I had often been struck by how the beauty of everything was magnified by sunshine. It was like nature's own Windex, washing everything to a sparkle, and rarely more so than on this morning.

Leaving the pond and starting to climb, I ran into a young guy, Dude, having a cigarette on the trail. He casually informed me that he had started on June 9, and was averaging over 25 miles a day. I had started 78 days before this kid and needed all my breath to make every mountain at a somewhat less striking pace. Here he was, puffing away like Thomas the Tank Engine, and eating up the ground like the Road Runner. I shook my head and waved him goodbye, in the absolute certainty that we'd never meet again. I was wrong, as he passed me—in a blur—about ten minutes later. Then I was right. *Meep, meep.*

Hikers were spared a boggy walk soon after by a magnificent, clearly new, wooden path through fields. These boardwalks could be in dramatically varying degrees of disrepair, yet this was almost pristine and very welcome.

A little later, I ran into Stardust, the young woman I'd met a few days before. She was sitting on a rock, crying her eyes out, sobbing that she was homesick. She wanted to go home, having lost her group, and was scared to hike and camp by herself. She thought she may have contracted Lyme disease, which was why she had gone into Rutland to find a doctor to check her out. The test had proved to be negative, and now she was scared and alone. While I wasn't scared, I was certainly alone. I recalled how close I'd come to quitting the day before, so I really felt for her, and tried to help her think rationally about it. I talked to her about heading back to the Inn at Long Trail, then waiting for another group of friends to catch up. I said I'd walk back with her if she'd like. She asked me which shelter I was heading for that day, so I told her. However, she was still undecided on what to do as I left. I doubted that I'd see her again. At the same time, I worried that perhaps I should have done more. As the day's hiking unfolded, I thought about Stardust, hoping that she would make the Wintturi Shelter, my target for the night.

Towards the end of this excellent hiking day, during which I covered 18 miles, I stopped to get some water from a stream. I couldn't find my filter. Panic quickly set in. I searched my entire pack before finding the filter precisely where it was supposed to be. Everything had to be in its place and, when an item seemed to be missing, my reaction was both immediate and negative.

I reached Wintturi Shelter, where I met a section hiker, Papa. He had started hiking the trail in sections on his retirement at 60. He was very chatty and eager to ask about doing the whole thing at once. There was another thru-hiker at the shelter. We were all chatting amiably when Stardust turned up, grinning at me, about 15 minutes later. She was clearly in a far more positive frame of mind and thanked me for talking her off the ledge.

Often, it is the small things that count and that have the most impact. I still worried that she might quit, but she looked far more composed that evening, so I hoped for the best. I'm sure that I helped Stardust that day, but she had already returned the favor. Seeing her vulnerability on the path allowed me to put my own woes of the past few days in perspective. Raising her spirits had raised my own, and I didn't return to those depths for the rest of my journey.

I slept far better than I had of late, waking at my 5:35 a.m. alarm. I had a chatty breakfast with Papa, and we were joined by Giblets, a section hiker I had met the previous evening. He had camped about three miles before the shelter. Giblets was a vegan and he showed us his breakfast. It was a combination of hydrated dried pineapple and bananas from Trader Joe's that looked predictably revolting, though it packed a gut-busting 1,100 calories.

Giblets and I left the shelter together. We saw each other several times through the day, passing one another as we stopped for various snacks. By now, I was shoveling Snickers, peanut butter, and wraps down my throat, while my healthy friend absorbed vegetables and fruit on a similar scale.

For some reason that day, the trail bore no apparent resemblance to my guide, so I was unaware how far I'd traveled. I was just beginning to think that I'd gone wrong again, when I spotted a farm shop—which was mentioned in my guide—about

300 yards off the trail. At the shop, I ran into three SOBOs and Giblets. I had a breakfast burrito, followed by blueberry and pecan pie with ice cream. I also treated myself to some cheese for later. As you may have gathered from my endless list of unhealthy food, my hunger was constant. In speaking with others, it seemed that this was going to last for about a month following the hike, so I fully expected to be a fat bloke again by my birthday at the end of October.

Soon after lunch, carrying my straining stomach up another hill, I ran into two familiar faces—Songbird and Bypass. I had last seen them about 1,000 miles before, yet here they were, coming towards me. They had flip-flopped, meaning that they had reached halfway, then gone to Katahdin and hiked south. They assured me that, while they were tough, Maine and New Hampshire were eminently "doable" and exciting to hike. I was happy to see them again, and it was reassuring to hear their assessment of my final two states.

I got to the Thistle Hill Shelter after a less than 12-mile day, meeting more SOBOs, variously named Spot, Chin Up, and Pickles. We were later joined by Giblets, Sonic, and Froggy Fellow, with his dog, Rocket Dog. Seeing Songbird and Bypass brought to mind all the people I had met on the trail to this point. It seemed appropriate and comforting to spend the evening at a full shelter, with everybody cooking and sharing food.

Giblets, who seemed to cater like a Puerto Rican, gave me a meal of black beans and rice. He also offered me his breakfast combo of bananas and pineapple, which I gratefully accepted and hydrated overnight. In case you were wondering exactly what catering like a Puerto Rican entails, let me explain. A Puerto Rican woman—when cooking for her husband, family, or friends—will always make a little extra on the vague chance that 20 of her relatives will turn up out of the blue looking for sustenance. Such advanced catering tends to result in endless leftovers as, believe it or not, 20 Puerto Ricans have never knocked on our door in the middle of the day. I could only presume that Giblets, out for a short section hike, was married to a Puerto Rican.

The following morning was a beauty, with the sun slowly, and blazingly, lighting up the east-facing shelter. As usual, I was awake and out of my tent first, while the others gradually came to. Amazingly, once we were all awake, we noticed that Giblets was still snoring in the shelter, with everybody, laughing, talking, cooking, and packing around him. He was like a noisy corpse, and only woke just as I was about to leave.

Without going into too much technical detail, my hydrated-fruit breakfast decided that it wanted no further part of me after about an hour, and I gave up 1,100 calories in the bushes. I am blessed with a system that quickly makes up its mind as to whether or not food is going to stay. In this case, the Trader Joe's stuff got the thumbs down, and the forest received some unplanned fertilizer. Shit happens, as they say.

I got to West Hartford, a tiny hamlet directly on the trail. A bridge crosses a lively river to reach the main drag. A woman pulled up in her car as I was crossing and pointed out her house. She told me that I could get coffee there. Never one to refuse a gift, I walked up to the house, to be greeted by a jolly guy named Randy. He and his wife, Linda—who turned out to be the lady in the car—welcomed hikers to their home for coffee, and breakfast, if they wanted it. This was something of a rhetorical question for me, so I stayed for about an hour while Randy kept putting pancakes and bacon in front of me. I figured that as long as he kept putting them there, I'd keep eating them.

He told me that his village had been devastated by Hurricane Irene a couple of years previously. The river had burst its banks and Randy's house had been under five feet of water. It was a dramatic story, imbued with hope by Randy and Linda's generous spirit to hikers.

I knew that I still had another nine miles to go before crossing the Connecticut River, where I would be passing into my penultimate state, New Hampshire. In the interim, there was the small issue of Griggs Mountain to pass over. Fortunately, the climb was undulating, though fairly mild, and, once at the top, the descent was very comfortable. I needed to pick up my pace towards the end because I was due to meet with the son of my friends from Connecticut, Brian and Dee, with whom I had stayed about 300 miles back. They also owned property in New Hampshire, and had invited me to come and stay with them again. They clearly hadn't had enough of their smelly friend. I was looking forward to seeing them.

I met Stewart in Hanover, and he drove me to his folks' house about 30 minutes away for my last zero day on the A.T.

Chapter 21: Into New Hampshire

With my zero days now in the past, Stewart drove me back to Starbucks, where he had met me two evenings before. Brian and Dee had let me simply relax, chat, and eat, all of which I was delighted to do, but I was now ready to get back at it. Of course, at Starbucks I couldn't resist the temptation of a triple, grande, non-fat latte and a blueberry scone. Old habits die hard—I should have had a triple, grande, full-fat latte. As a consequence, I dallied for 30 minutes before hitting the trail once more. It was spitting with intermittent rain, and didn't feel like a great start to the day.

Soon, what rain there was eased off. My first impression of hiking in New Hampshire was that it was all fairly benign. There was a gentle uphill to begin with, but nothing too terrifying. I knew that this was an entirely false impression but enjoyed deluding myself nonetheless. My mantra for these early miles, in my most-dreaded states, seemed to be that until I had to face it, I would convince myself that I'd be okay.

I ran into a couple of familiar faces that morning. First, there was Voodoo. She was the young woman who had witnessed my most embarrassing moment on the trail. We chatted over a snack for a few minutes before moving on. I saw no indication on her face that she had seen what could not be unseen. I'm not entirely sure if that thought made me feel better or worse.

The second, and the most significant person I met on that gray morning, just into New Hampshire, was Lighterknot. He was the guy in his 50s who I'd camped beside in Connecticut. Reintroducing ourselves, we soon discovered that we had similar outlooks. We even talked about possibly teaming up for some of the tougher climbs to come. Both of us felt that safety in numbers might be preferable at this stage, while we also both mentioned the loneliness on the trail. We agreed to meet later at Moose Mountain Shelter, then decide where to end the day.

It is only now, writing this more than a year after we first met, that I have realized how serendipitous our meetings had been. The first time we had met had been back in Connecticut. I had spent the previous evening with my friends, Brian and Dee. Three hundred miles had since passed. Now, just 30 minutes into my day, having spent the night with Brian and Dee for the second time—and in a different state—Lighterknot and I had run into one another once more. Even more providential was the fact that I'd delayed my start by about 30 minutes at Starbucks. I tended to walk slightly faster than Lighterknot, so I may well have missed him if I'd rejoined the trail immediately.

I've rarely been so grateful for a cup of coffee.

By the time we got to the shelter the rain was just starting to take hold. So we decided that our day was over after only 11 miles by 3 o'clock. A quiet Japanese guy who Lighterknot had met before, Loon, joined us later. We were all settled in our sleeping bags in the shelter by 7:30. I didn't like using shelters, but the rain was intense, so I made an exception.

While the rain itself subsided, throughout the night the wind blew spray from the trees on to the shelter, drowning out any mouse or chipmunk activity, which was fine by me. They may have been marching round like a bunch of noisy kids in kindergarten, poking into our packs, though as long as I couldn't hear them, I was good to go.

I had probably my best night in a shelter, waking refreshed and ready to move on. I was out by 7:50, making excellent progress for the first five miles. The real mountains were still to come, yet I had noticed sharper inclines as we pushed further north. I struggled for the rest of the day to make another seven miles.

Unlike the mountains in the South, these tended to be pretty much straight up, with no side-to-side. I had to take extensive breaks, gasping to regain both my breath and the power in my legs. That said, I took heart from the undeniable fact that, pain and anguish notwithstanding, there hadn't been a single mountain I'd failed to get over. More than any other, this realization always gave me the confidence to look the upcoming terrain directly in the eye, and tell both it and myself that I'd eventually be at the top. As luck would have it, I always turned out to be right.

Lighterknot and I stopped at the amiable Bill Ackerly's home, just after the Lyme-Dorchester road. Bill had put a cute homemade sign out to attract hikers, promising free ice cream and water top-up. Naturally, the place had attracted several old and new faces, all eager to avail themselves of Bill's hospitality. A few were still on his porch from the night before.

Bill was a real gent, delighted to have hikers cluttering up his porch and slurping down ice cream. He claimed that it was his eighty-sixth birthday, though one of the hikers who had been there the previous evening said that he had said the same thing the day before. He was an absolute treat to meet.

After a tough climb of about 2,000 feet, I got to our target shelter, the Firewarden's Cabin, which was a very dreary, closed building. I didn't fancy staying in it at all, so I waited for Lighterknot before we settled on a tenting site. We found a small clearing, a few hundred yards before the shelter, with a spectacular view to the valley below. I had my best sleep in a tent in a long while, and we breakfasted the next morning with our glorious view directly in front of us.

Lighterknot left ten minutes before me and stopped at the shelter, where he found Loon. We arranged to meet at Ore Hill, about 12 miles away, so I tried to make some early progress down the hill, which was wet, rocky, and very muddy. Indeed, I fell for the twenty-seventh, twenty-eighth, and twenty-ninth time. Each time, I slipped on the mud, with all the falls occurring within an hour. I didn't hurt myself, but falling always slowed me down. It also made me more tentative—though clearly not tentative enough—for I continued my fall-fest throughout both New Hampshire and Maine.

I ran into several SOBOs, many of whom were eager to share their stories of the White Mountains and Maine. The whole thing sounded like a bit of a horror story to me, and, for the first time, I felt that I might miss my September 25 target date. Diane always told me that she would rather I missed her birthday and stayed safe, so I resolved to concentrate on the safety while still keeping an eye on the miles per day. I hadn't given up my goal, but I knew that I needed to get to the end if all of this was going to be the achievement I wanted it to be. I knew I'd already done an remarkable thing, but to finish on a fall would have been devastating. My focus fell even more clearly upon that photograph at the top of Katahdin.

Despite falling three times on this day, the climbs were nothing I hadn't experienced before, and I got to the camp at Ore Hill by about 4 o'clock. Lighterknot showed up about 30 minutes later, while Loon rolled in at about 6:30. I had spent nearly 1,800 miles concerned about how slow I was to get moving in the mornings, yet Loon made me look positively sprightly. He never seemed in a hurry to get anywhere, though when he got going, he was faster than both me and Lighterknot.

I must say, knowing that I wouldn't be camping alone anymore was a good feeling, so I hoped I had found the partners I had been previously avoiding. I had already learned—and here was another example—of the need to be fluid in your plans on the Appalachian Trail. Almost overnight I had gone from a complete aversion to hiking partners to welcoming them into my hike. With my two new amigos around me, I slept well again, waking at 6:20 a.m., refreshed and ready to go.

Having teamed up, our threesome almost immediately became a twosome. Loon developed different plans from Lighterknot and me, but the three of us decided to hike just eight miles into Glencliff the following morning for a couple of reasons. First, I had a food pick-up from the Glencliff Post Office. I was now down to my last few Snickers, and in desperate need of more. The opening hours had been changed, I was told, so I was anxious to make sure I was there during the short window the post office would be open. Second, Mount Moosilauke was the beginning of the White Mountains, and Lighterknot and I wanted to slackpack our first mountain in that range. Looking at the profile of Moosilauke, a north-to-south route appeared to be the easier way to go.

Lighterknot, Loon, and I got to the road at NH25 at the same time. We then headed east, reaching the Hikers Welcome Hostel within half a mile. It was rather like Standing Bear

Farm—which had been more than 1,000 miles back—where nothing looked right but it all worked. A shower, laundry, tent site, and shopping trip allowed us all to hang out for the afternoon, chatting with SOBOs and one guy who was boomeranging. Apparently, he had started on Springer Mountain the same day as me, had already been to Katahdin, and was heading back to Springer. Extraordinary!

I was really looking forward to Moosilauke the following morning and, with a forecast for great weather for the next five days, everything was set fair for the Whites. How little I knew what I was about to experience.

Many miles behind me, an experienced hiker had said that the moment I stepped above the trees in New Hampshire would be the moment I'd realize why I was hiking the Appalachian Trail. I was always skeptical of such hyperbole, though he turned out to be right on the money.

Lighterknot and I had taken the opportunity to slackpack over Moosilauke in order to save our knees. The Hikers Welcome Hostel was also a cheap and cheerful place to stay for a second night, so several other hikers joined us. It would be fair to say that we were all more than a little intimidated by the mountain's reputation. However, the difference when carrying such a depleted pack was so liberating. As we walked, views started to unfold, and we appreciated those lighter packs.

Suddenly, emerging above the tree line, we were able to absorb our vast surroundings for the first time. A young guy in a kilt, Shepherd, was snapping away at straggling hikers with his camera. He had reached a rocky outcrop near the summit, perching himself upon it to record the contented faces of exhaustion as they passed him. There were about 20 people at the top, many of whom I knew, and we all sat around in the idyllic sun having lunch for about 90 minutes.

Walking down with Lighterknot a short time later, I had my thirtieth fall, slipping on a root. With my bear-scaring whistle in my back pocket, it really hurt my backside. Despite the fact that the whistle was relatively impotent in its rusty state, I had been loath to part with it. During the day, I'd remarked to Lighterknot that it would be great to be able to slackpack all the way to Maine. An idea started to form.

When I got to the bottom, I suggested that we could each offer to pay somebody about $250 to manage this for us. With a team of four, it could prove to be an interesting proposition to a hard-up hiker. Looking back at how patronizing that reads, I'm afraid I can only chalk it up to the benefit of being of more advanced years, and marginally less impecunious than some. As it turned out, I had hit upon a scheme that appealed to others and allowed several of us to make our journey easier than it might otherwise have been. We also found somebody who didn't seem to feel in the least bit patronized. So, everybody had an upside.

Many miles before, I had run into Tee Bird, hiking with a husband and wife couple. At the time, I was recovering from yet another fall. I had joined them in search of a drink, to no avail, and had bumped into Tee Bird several times over the miles since then. She was now hiking on her own, because the married couple had quit the trail. Tee Bird had suggested once or twice that we could team up to hike together. That had never happened, but she was staying at the hostel that evening. She was now hiking with Trillium, a woman in her early 40s. We spoke to the two women about our idea and they seemed responsive. I think we had all reached the stage where we knew that the danger was increasing exponentially. We all wanted some security to help us achieve our respective goals.

Trillium happened to know Shepherd, the young guy who had been photographing hikers at the top of Moosilauke earlier in the day. He was already spending much of his time both hiking and helping hikers, so we put our financial proposal to him. Without committing to how much he could help, or how much cash he might want, we were able to shed some weight to leave in Shepherd's truck.

The next few days weren't going to be complete slackpacks. We couldn't meet up with Shepherd every day, so we needed a larger supply of food, along with most of the rest of our gear. My pack became a far more appealing proposition at 30 pounds and, while it wasn't as great as the day before, it was appreciably more comfortable than my everyday burden.

Our team was formed and we were into the Whites.

Chapter 22: The Whites and the Presidentials

So, with the four of us carrying lighter loads the following morning, Shepherd dropped us back at Kinsman Notch at the spot where Lighterknot and I had turned southward the previous day to cross Moosilauke. We were now heading north once more. The early pace was certainly down, though this was more in recognition of the changing, and more dramatic, topography, which seemed to threaten us with each turning page of our guidebooks.

It was another day of tough climbs and grand views, crossing Mount Wolf before dipping down again. Then, we steadily climbed the sensational South Kinsman Mountain, only for a short dip down, back up, then over North Kinsman Mountain. All the while, we marveled at what we were seeing.

I've often wondered if I had tried to do this hike from north to south whether or not my spirit would have been broken by Maine or New Hampshire. My hiking legs were now allowing me to get over these massive rocks, having earned that strength from the many miles behind me. However, the entire experience in these last two states seemed to be what we had come here for. Georgia to Vermont had turned out to be our warm-up states. I'm not sure I could have coped had I chosen the alternative.

Trillium struggled with her knees all day, and Tee Bird hiked with her for most of the time. Lighterknot went ahead to meet up with some friends who were visiting him on the trail. I hiked alone, though this time I was content to be by myself. I knew that we'd all be meeting up later and that gave me a lot of comfort.

Eventually, after an 11-mile day, we gathered again at Kinsman Pond Shelter. To my dismay, Kinsman Pond was the water source and, once I'd collected it, the water looked very much like a urine specimen. Despite a not-unnatural reticence, I filtered and cooked with it. Everything tasted fine, though I'd imagine my standards may have slipped a touch by this stage.

New Hampshire was a pay-to-stay state, so we had to hand over eight bucks each to the caretaker for a spot of real estate that could barely hold four tents. It was away from the shelter, and we were very much back in the woods. We were cramped, but glad to be together.

This had been my best day hiking to this point, with plenty of clambering hand-over-hand, a style with which I became quickly comfortable, greatly overcoming my fear of the White Mountains. That record only lasted overnight, for the following day blasted aside everything that had gone before.

Coming to New England held the prospect of seeing moose for the first time, yet many hikers told us not to expect too much. We had seen nothing in those earlier miles, and this seemed like solid advice. Apparently, moose tend to keep out of the way of hikers, so I put such an encounter to the back of my mind.

Leaving Kinsman Pond behind, we were heading down to Franconia Notch to restock from Shepherd, before starting up towards Franconia Ridge. We were somewhere around Lonesome Lake Hut, walking very close together. We were chatting away, with me in front of our line. Planks had been placed on the ground as the trail was a bit boggy, while the forest was especially deep at this point. Ahead, no more than 30 paces in front of us, was an adult bull moose. I saw him first, and was temporarily taken aback, as much by his sheer size as anything else. I put my hand up. The others stopped. The moose was munching away on the trail, showing no indication of having seen or heard us. He didn't move. Normally, I was far too slow to get my camera into gear, but this was clearly a cooperative moose who hung about long enough even for my sloth-like reactions. As I was shooting a short video, Lighterknot had pulled out his camera. The resulting picture of me filming the moose showed how uncomfortably close I was. Since the beast was showing no inclination to move away, we all watched in

awe. It was a special moment; we'd been privileged to have witnessed it. Eventually, having taken his fill of leaves, he ambled down the path before heading back into the forest. I was able to take a terrific shot of him from behind, showing the unmitigated power of his legs.

Moose may not be the most beautiful of animals, though, for me, they have an undeniable air of belonging to another time. I was thrilled to have seen one with Maine still to come.

It was soon after this that I ran into Shepherd. He was out for a morning hike and knew that he would eventually meet up with us. He had left his truck down at Franconia Notch and was doing a swift 17-miler all the way back to Kinsman Notch. From there, he planned to hitch back to his truck. I was exhausted even listening to his active life, and I loved his attitude towards the vicissitudes of life on the trail.

He wanted to let us know where he had parked his truck, and how to get into it, so he gave me clear instructions. "When you get to the bridge at the bottom, instead of crossing the bridge, keep on the path, then take a right turn, about half-a-mile further on, and that path will lead to the car park where I left the truck."

I repeated the highlights. "Miss out the bridge, right turn about half mile on, path to car park. Got it."

The others caught up at this point, so Shepherd repeated his instructions. I echoed them once more. "Bridge, right after half mile, path to truck. Excellent."

Having heard or repeated these instructions four times, I was fairly confident that I knew the way. For some reason, Trillium seemed to doubt this. We reached the bridge as a group and I said, "Right, it's down this way."

Trillium piped up. "Wait a minute, where are you going?"

While I recognize the cliché about men never listening to instructions, I felt that I was on safe ground, so I reiterated that this was the right way. Trillium was not to be deterred and said "I certainly didn't hear that," once I'd repeated Shepherd's instructions. "Now Mighty Blue, you may be used to women listening to you and hanging on your every word, but I'm not one of those women. You need to listen."

I'm afraid that my patronizing gear clicked in at this point, as I knew with a certainty that I had given the correct directions. "You're absolutely right," I said, slowly choosing my words. "I should listen more, and I'd be delighted if you would tell us all which way we should be going. Mind you, once you're done, I'm going this way, because this is the right bloody way." I turned and walked off.

    Lighterknot and Tee Bird had diplomatically held their silence and followed me, as did Trillium, her face crimson with rage. I'd like to say that I felt bad about this testy exchange, but I'm afraid I didn't. She seemed determined not to agree with me on most issues in those early days. We often fell out, though never seriously, and she didn't appear to hold a grudge. She always had plenty to say for herself, as did I, so I suppose we were likely to clash. Early on, I told Lighterknot that if you asked Trillium the time, she'd tell you how to make a watch. I used to say this about an old friend in the U.K., and I could hear Lighterknot laughing his quiet, deep Georgia laugh for several minutes at the inherent truth in this statement.

    Astonishingly, the truck was precisely where I thought it would be. I think that simply smiling at Trillium at that point would have been sufficient. Instead, unable to hold back, I innocently muttered, "Good lord, here it is. Who'd have thunk?" The crimson took on a deeper hue, and she didn't say a word for 15 minutes, breaking her previous record by at least ten minutes.

    Franconia Ridge links a number of consecutive peaks, including Mount Liberty and Mount Lincoln. I had neither experienced nor imagined anything like it in my life. As we climbed higher, we suddenly emerged above the tree line. The sight truly took my breath away. I knew it was coming up, and I had seen pictures, though nothing prepared me for the pure excitement that I felt. I can only equate that moment with going on a skiing vacation for the first time, and riding up in a cable car. I knew what snow looked like, and I knew what mountains looked like. However, the magical combination of the two produced something almost other-worldly that completely overwhelmed me.

Coming out of those trees did it again and I felt like a kid once more. Indeed, I unashamedly giggled like one. The whole area looked like a moonscape and I was an astronaut. It was harsh, it was spectacular, and, with 360-degree views for miles, it overwhelmed me. Even my first skiing trip slid down a notch on my list of lifetime jaw-droppers.

On the top of Mount Lincoln, I got sufficient signal to FaceTime Diane, so much did I want to share my emotions with her. I knew that this was a pivotal moment in my journey, and I just wanted to have her with me, albeit via a cell signal.

The wind was whipping around, but this just enhanced the pleasure for me, with the wildness exhilarating and testing in equal measure. On the way down, I was with Trillium, who was getting a little scared. The wind was gusting so much that it was pushing us into the rocks at the side of the trail, so it was a very tricky descent in rapidly downward-spiraling temperatures.

After a long, though wonderfully satisfying day, we found a stealth-camping site at Garfield Pond. News of stealth sites seemed to circulate amongst hikers along the trail as spots that could be camped at unofficially. There was no apparent area in which to pitch our tents nor, of course, a privy, although we had been told where to look. We found a good-sized clearing back in the woods, about 50 yards off the trail. Once more, water was sourced from the pond, though this time it was the correct color. It was also the coldest night I'd experienced since the Smokies, and retrieving water was an urgent necessity as the light died. The others had quickly retired to their tents as I cooked alone, in the cold and dark forest. I remember smiling to myself, almost perversely, as I felt, probably for the first time, that I was a genuine hiker. I was cold, I was dirty, I was uncomfortable, and I was deep in the forest. Such a realization had been a while taking hold, but it was there, and I don't think I've lost it to this day.

The cold night that followed was a bit of a shock to the system, so it was still all cold-weather clothing in the morning.

We were aiming for another stealth site, just after Zealand Falls Hut, but first, we had to negotiate Mount Garfield.

It was quite an uphill scramble, though my newfound confidence over the rocks was certainly helping. I could feel my hiking improving with each step. While the climb up was a scramble, the climb down tested our balance, with the severity of slope examining us all.

Once more, I spent quite a bit of the day with Trillium, who continued to struggle with her knees, particularly following such a tough slog the day before. Consequently, we kept a fairly slow pace, though managed to achieve our goal. Lighterknot was also suffering with his knees from the previous day.

Trillium was a combative character, though I learned later that she had a very good reason to be so. She and I would often clash, though she never once failed to reach the target we had set, and we kept up quite a pace through the Whites. She would bitch and moan when a new target was suggested, but she always got there by the end of the day. We may have often been at odds, but I admired her tenacity.

We reached Zealand Falls Hut, one of the group of New Hampshire huts that hikers can, well, beg for food by asking for "work for scraps." I got there first. The young man in charge put me to work scrubbing a filthy baking tin that looked like it had never seen soap before. I tried hard, though made scant impression on the grime. My young boss seemed quite satisfied with my efforts, giving me a bowl of cold oatmeal with raisins, followed by potato soup, both of which I dispatched with alacrity. I also bought a couple of chocolate-chip cakes and woofed them down as well.

When we had all scoffed down our free food, we moved on to a terrific stealth site only about a couple of miles past the hut. There was a large clearing, with several other clearings adjacent to it. Our fellow hikers had already set up for the night. The weather had improved, so we spent a far warmer evening hanging out with each other, and our neighbors. We had quite the village once more.

The next morning was the easiest day so far in New Hampshire. It was generally downhill all the way, and we were only going about eight miles to meet up with Shepherd again. We were planning to find a motel to clean both ourselves and our clothes.

Straight after we started, I reached into my pack for my ibuprofen and dropped my entire stock all over the trail. Vitamin I had been my constant companion for months by now. Two in the morning with breakfast, followed by two at lunchtime, and my aching joints felt sufficiently oiled so as not to impinge upon my enjoyment of each day. I was horrified when they fell, for, quite apart from my need for these wonder pills, I didn't wish to be responsible for the death of any unsuspecting critters, so I spent 20 minutes scrambling around on the trail to make sure that each one was recovered.

A terrific Trail Magic session was set up at the bottom. I enjoyed, among many things, two fried eggs. Eggs were a treat beyond expectations. We hung around chatting and chomping in the late morning sunshine. Here we found Heike, a middle-aged German hiker we'd run into before. She joined us as Shepherd drove us to find a place to spend the night. We eventually came to the Seven Dwarfs Motel, a sort of run down Disney-themed place that checked all the right boxes. The three girls shared a room, while Lighterknot and I had a room each. When they had already shared a shelter with several farting, snoring, and generally revolting men, I'd imagine the girls were sufficiently content to bunk in together to avoid that delight.

Shepherd was so patient, taking us down into the village for a late lunch, then moving us on to a grocery store to re-provision. Back at the Seven Dwarfs, we set about washing our clothes in the sink, which was something of a departure for me. I may have overindulged myself with the soap somewhat, because everything was a bit slimy when I hung it all out to dry overnight, though it seemed okay to me in the morning. However, I may be a touch behind the curve when it comes to judging these things.

The Presidential Range was another of those marquee moments that I'd been looking forward to, but couldn't really imagine.

The Seven Dwarfs Motel was hardly the place to set out from if you're going to take on this magnificent range of mountains, each lifting you higher in terms of not only altitude but also superlatives. The motel sat at about 1,500 feet, while the climb ahead was going to take us, ultimately, to Mount Washington, at just under 6,500 feet.

For this day we had set our sights on the Lakes of the Clouds Hut, which was at about 5,200 feet and another 11 miles along the trail. We knew that we'd have to cross mounts Webster, Jackson, Clinton, and Franklin on the way. The Presidential Range was saving Mount Washington for the following morning.

The initial climb out of the valley was a bit of a mission in itself, climbing nearly 2,000 feet in only two miles, with unfolding views accompanying us. There was a very negative forecast, which ultimately proved to be correct, as the clouds closed in near the top and all views disappeared. I was invigorated by those early miles, but so disappointed to see the clouds roll in. In the end, we were slogging along in about 30 feet of visibility, eventually making the Lakes of the Clouds Hut by about 4 o'clock. One big regret of my entire journey was the fact that I missed those views. I'd love one day to do the whole Presidential Range again.

Another sour note was that I fell once more. Unfortunately, on the fall I snapped one of my trusty poles as I landed. You may recall, back in Virginia that I had left my previous set of poles in a car. I had been lucky enough to buy a used set from Lover Boy, a hiker who was injured and on his way home. I told him at the time that he may not get to Katahdin but his poles would. A small part of me felt that I'd let him down, though I was grateful to have taken the poles as far as I had. Breaking stuff on the trail is part of the deal; you just have to make sure that you don't break your body or your mind. My poles had become an integral part of me. They acted as extra legs, and the difference hiking with just the one was noticeable.

Quite how anybody ever managed without poles was beyond me. I knew that I'd be getting another pair as soon as I could.

The Lakes of the Clouds Hut had a reputation of being one of the friendliest huts in New Hampshire. Despite a few reservations, we were treated well. The hut system was quite unlike anything we had experienced. We had been used to crummy shelters and clearings in the wood, but, frankly, we were all fine with that. These huts were more like lodges based on a European model, run by the Appalachian Mountain Club. They were aimed at the day hikers in the White Mountains. These people would hike the 56 miles covered by the eight huts, one hut at a time, paying over $100 each night to stay and be fed. I could entirely see the attraction in this arrangement.

Of course, if you mix Appalachian Trail hikers into this social gathering, certain standards are going to drop. We were made to feel like interlopers. I understand the need to fund these places. I can also see that their prime market isn't going to be a bunch of smelly beggars cluttering up the place. However, staying in these lodges provided all of us thru-hikers with a glimpse of exclusion that I'm sure many outsiders have felt over the years. I may be a little over-sensitive here, but I never saw a raising of the flag when we arrived, bedraggled and wet.

We were able to stay in the hut overnight by doing "work for stay." This variant of "work for scraps" involved more work, including endless washing up—by Trillium and me, in a sink designed for a midget—and fridge cleaning which, according to Tee Bird and Lighterknot, was way past overdue.

We were certainly fed well, and were allowed to sleep in the dining room, in most cases on the floor. I was able to snag a bench, eventually settling down for what proved to be a disturbed night.

Everybody was dreading first light, as we knew the tenor of the day would be set by the weather conditions. The climb up Mount Washington was immediately in front of us, and we were keenly aware of its ferocious reputation.

The weather on Washington is dangerously erratic, with a wind speed of 231 mph recorded at the top, nearly a century ago. This was an eye-popping and focus-inducing number that rattled around inside our heads as we faced the prospect of climbing it. We were also aware that nearly 150 people had died on the mountain, so we were particularly focused when we looked out of the hut window the following morning, to be confronted by thick cloud.

We settled back to wait and see how things would develop. Within ten minutes there were small breaks in the cloud and we made the collective decision to go. The four of us were among the first to head out from the hut that morning. We never regretted the decision.

I had been hiking so much better in the Whites and the Presidentials and set off like a train, pushing on as the path revealed itself in front of me. We had braved the early doubts over what the cloud was going to do, then were rewarded as the sun burst through. The beauty opened up all around us, like a painting revealed, bit by bit, for the first time. I was filming at that moment. I often watch the resulting short video, listening to my wild, almost childlike excitement. As much as anything else, it seemed to confirm that the weather was going to cooperate with us, so my excitement contained more than a touch of gratitude for our safe passage. We were still wary of the weather closing in on us. There had been snow the day before at the summit, so we pushed on to make sure that we took advantage of our good fortune.

The wind was whipping around at the top and, after a quick team snap, we found the snack bar. Inside, we topped up our sugar and calorie levels once we'd savored the joy of getting to the top. It seemed shockingly surreal to come out of the wind into a warm, comfortable snack bar and we took full opportunity to recharge our phones, while overdosing on calories. By now, the view had been hidden by cloud once more so, given the unpredictability of the weather, we moved on. We were heading for the next hut and, ultimately, the Osgood Tentsite.

Trillium and Lighterknot were hiking slower than me and Tee Bird that day. However, we all relished the noticeably milder temperatures and occasional break in the cloud as the day unfolded. I reached the top of Mount Adams and waited for my companions to join me before heading down again to another hut. The daunting-looking Mount Madison, our after-lunch target, was constantly in our sight. It looked like the type of mountain I used to draw as a five-year-old: a triangle coming to a precise point at the top. At the Madison Spring Hut we lunched inside and braced ourselves for the steep climb up Madison and the following, far longer, descent.

I don't know what it was about that day, or that mountain, but I shot ahead on another exhilarating climb that saw me at the top quite a while before the others. There was plenty of hand-over-hand scrambling that was right in my wheelhouse. I surged ahead. The tiny perch I found at the summit gave me a dramatic, though precarious, 360-degree view of my surroundings, and the mountain even felt like the one I had in mind as a five-year-old. The descent from Madison was probably the toughest we'd had to handle so far, climbing down nearly 3,500 feet in just shy of three miles, feeling like at least four times that distance. It was absolutely dreadful and everybody's knees took a pounding.

Lighterknot and I had reached the Osgood Tentsite and had set up before the two girls arrived. As they came in, at least 40 minutes later, I was perhaps a little over-cheery. Trillium had rather lost her sense of humor by this point. Her scowl and curt words cut me off, so we had a quiet evening and crashed early. I was rarely one to be shut up by a scowling woman, though Trillium glared so thunderously at me that I decided this was to be a rare exception. Call me old-fashioned, but sometimes you just need to keep your mouth shut. You probably won't be shocked when I tell you that this had never been a skill that came easily to me.

It had been a wonderful, tough, exhilarating, brutal day that tested all of us. However, we had completed a major part of the White Mountains—including the Presidential Range—without injury. Because of the severity of some of the climbs and, indeed, some of the descents, we had only been able to cover about 11 miles a day. We had taken about ten or 11 hours of hard hiking, every day, to achieve this. I knew that there was plenty of tough stuff to come, but my sense of achievement that night allowed me to sleep soundly. Katahdin loomed ever closer, dominating my thoughts as I dropped off.

My Appalachian Trial II: Creaking Geezer, Hidden Flagon

Chapter 23: Out of New Hampshire

Pinkham Notch was our first target the following morning. We had arranged to meet Shepherd once more and refill our food bags. The terrain didn't seem too bad, with only the wonderfully named Lowe's Bald Spot to get over, though I struggled all the way. I was glad to get there, even though it was less than five miles. That said, we made it in under three hours. We immediately hit the snack bar for a very substantial sandwich and various sweet goodies before consolidating our food bags.

You may recall that I had talked a young woman, Stardust, "off the ledge," when she was contemplating quitting in Vermont. I was filled with almost paternal pride when I saw her that morning, at Pinkham Notch, smiling and hiking with a bunch of friends. Even better, a few months later—while looking through some finishing pictures online for the Class of 2014 thru-hikers—I saw her joyous celebration at the top of Katahdin. I couldn't help thinking that I'd played a part in her success, albeit very minor, as others had done in getting me to this point. If you ever take the opportunity to hike the trail, you should be prepared for unexpected benevolence that will be coming your way. It is balm for the soul.

    I had been trying to make do with a single trekking pole but, having got used to both, I was struggling. So I splashed out $100 to buy a decent set of Leki poles. The effect was immediate, and I got stuck into the hike up from Pinkham Notch. We had a substantial climb to the first of the Wildcat Mountain peaks, Peak D, with C, B, and A following the line of the ridge, before a steep, hair-raising downhill mile to Carter Notch Hut.

    This was the last of the A.M.C. huts, and it turned out to be one of the friendliest. We offered to "work for stay" but, with only one guest, they didn't need us to work but allowed us to sleep on the floor. There were eventually seven of us crammed into the dining room, so I grabbed two benches, put them together, and used them for my luxurious bed. Despite this extravagant self-indulgence, I spent another fairly sleepless night. I was grateful when the morning light seeped through the windows. We had to be packed up by 6:30 a.m. and out of the hut by 7 o'clock, just in case the single guest had the misfortune to actually set eyes upon us. As a result, we were hiking early on what turned out to be a great mileage day, though one that was stressful on all our legs.

The first climb, to the top of Carter Dome, was the most intense of the day, with about 1,500 feet of elevation gain in just over a mile. There was plenty of tough hand-over-hand stuff, though we all made it without too much trouble. We were then rewarded with absolutely no view once we got to the top, thanks to the blanketing cloud cover.

For the next couple of hours we were moving along the ridge, intermittently up and down, before we came to North Carter Mountain, with its truly ferocious descent on the north side. It was an unwelcome treat that was basically sheets of rock, wet from the overnight rain, and ready to catch us if we lost our concentration. I led the way, trying to find the least dangerous route down by a combination of rock handholds and footholds, tree trunks, branches, and even exposed roots, along with a heavy slice of luck. There were several times that I slipped, but I was always able to recover sufficiently to steady myself. I was able to help the others, as they helped me. I found it exhilarating, though it was playing havoc with both my knees. Our team was jelling well by now. I was grateful that we had chosen to end this adventure together.

We eventually made it to the beginning of the blue-blazed trail into Imp Shelter, where we perched on a couple of rocks and had lunch together. While we were sitting there, along came a couple of hikers I hadn't seen for several weeks, Hobo Nobo and Caddyshack. I loved running into old friends, often many miles after we had first met. The trail seemed to generate such serendipity on a regular basis.

Over lunch, we decided to push on to the Rattle River Shelter, which involved a climb up and over Mount Moriah, followed by another long downhill that we knew would further stress our legs. Trillium and Lighterknot were struggling by the time we eventually got to the shelter. We decided we'd camp there, then take the following day as a "nero," with just a few miles into town. We could then treat ourselves to an afternoon of rest and a night in a hostel.

For me, this was a significant decision, as it pretty much put my September 25 finish beyond me. I reasoned that hiking a wee bit slower with a team was far safer than hiking faster by myself. It was disappointing, though probably sensible. I squared the decision with both myself and Diane on one of our nightly calls. We both wanted this to be a life-affirming trip as opposed to a life-threatening one.

Another safe night, and we were marching on the way out of the White Mountains with hardly a scratch. We had enjoyed incredible luck with the weather, with heavy rain only coming when we were safely tucked up in huts or our tents. I shuddered to think how difficult these mountains would be if there was constant rain and the rocks were always slick.

At this stage of the hike, my diet was all about loading up on as many calories as possible, at every opportunity. I started buying one, two or even three jars of peanut butter at a time, with a jar sometimes not even making it beyond lunchtime.

Trillium also gave me a useful tip when she told me of a conversation she had had with a nutritionist. I had been munching on four high-protein bars a day, and her received theory was that this was the wrong time to be eating protein bars. A better way would be to change to Snickers or Cliff Bars through the day then, once hiking was over, go with the protein bars. Apparently, such a large protein intake, while walking, causes large amounts of wind. However, since men rarely concern themselves with the origins of their copious gas—indeed, are often proud of it—I hadn't connected the two. Of course, I rolled my eyes when Trillium started expounding upon my wind, as she rarely limited herself once she got going on a subject. In this case, she turned out to be spot on and I appreciated her intervention.

It was only a two-mile, downhill jaunt the following morning to US2, where we quickly found the White Mountains Lodge and Hostel, almost adjacent to the trailhead. It was a typical New England colonial home. The original house was built in 1877, with multiple additions since then. The place was a delight for me, with the first encouraging sign before we stepped over the threshold.

Hikers entered through the garage with Marni, the owner, directing with the efficiency of an air traffic controller. The first thing to do was to get out of your boots, shove your backpack in the corner, then dispense with your disgusting clothes. She wouldn't allow hikers into her home and, really, who could blame her? This latter instruction was complied with behind a curtain, where we put on the somewhat bohemian, but clean clothes provided by Marni herself, who washed our clothes overnight.

Being gentlemen, Lighterknot and I offered first dibs to Tee Bird and Trillium. Tee Bird came out shortly after, having taken about a minute to get out of and into her clothes, so it was Trillium's turn. Thirty seconds passed, then a minute, then two. I couldn't resist it, so I started hurrying her up, which I knew would tweak her a little. "Come on Trillium, it's not a fashion show, come on girl." As expected, she didn't take it at all well, cursing and spluttering before emerging, looking daggers at me.

It was my turn and I'd made something of a rod for my own back, feeling obliged to get in and out in record time. My  haste resulted in a look that could fairly be referred to as "hobo chic." Ditching everything, I grabbed the first large items I could find, then emerged looking like a refugee at the border. The picture that Lighterknot took of me in my new ensemble is one of my favorite pictures of the entire trip. Our version of fashion potluck encouraged some hikers to indulge in a bit of cross-dressing, for there were certainly some questionable choices out there. It was doubtless liberating to blame your selection on restricted availability.

Lighterknot and I were shown to what I referred as the David Hasselhoff Suite, so called because of the life-sized picture of "The Hoff" on the wall. Hopefully, it had been placed there by some pre-pubescent teen. That said, it was a comfortable room with a real bed and clean sheets, for which we were both very grateful. The fact that it was also used as a thoroughfare between rooms didn't dampen our spirits in the least; in fact, it added to the collegial atmosphere.

Marni, and her mom, Molly, were fabulous, tolerant hosts. They made us all feel welcome, driving us into town to stock up on food, then contentedly waiting as we made every effort to empty the store.

Later that evening, following a leisurely afternoon spent mangling a pizza in town, about a dozen contented souls sat scattered around the living room. A video was playing, accompanied by intermittent congenial chatter.

I was slumped in an armchair and took in the scene, closing my eyes after a full scan of the room. The warmth drew me deeper into the armchair and I allowed myself to think once more of the goal. We were only 17 miles short of the last state, and my desperation to finish felt like a nagging toothache. It simply wouldn't slide into the back of my mind, lying there as the backdrop to every decision I made. My falls had continued, increased even, although I always seemed able to recover and march on. That evening, with the warmth trying to comfort me, I came about as close as I've ever been to a panic attack. I was worrying about the next fall and my ability to get up. Shaking my head vigorously, in an attempt to literally shake this negative thought from my mind, I managed to calm down and smiled to myself. I thought back on the Whites and Presidential Range. I had been hiking well, and only needed to keep going for another 300 miles. As I'd asked myself several times before, what could possibly go wrong?

Breakfast at Marni's was a busy, noisy affair, with bacon, eggs, pancakes, and coffee in abundance. Our hostess knew what hit the spot, and supplied it accordingly. Her hostel had been a gem, and had set us up perfectly as we started what felt like the final leg of our journey.

With the Whites now behind us, we took some relief from the gentler incline at the start of the day. I should clarify that gentler is merely a relative term, not to be interpreted as gentle in any way. We were all sweating profusely within minutes, partly due to the incline, though mainly due to the warmth and humidity. Of course, the higher we got, the cooler it became. We managed to cover six miles before stopping for lunch at the top of Cascade Mountain.

We had all shopped feverishly at Walmart the previous evening, so we went about reducing our increased load by consuming as much as possible. By now, I was eating as many as six Snickers bars and a tub of peanut butter in a day, quite apart from my breakfast, lunch and dinner. Even now, every time I write "peanut butter" I want to get a spoonful from my larder.

Given the differing ambitions and capabilities of our group of four, we had to adjust the length of our potential mileage every day. On this day, we settled for Gentian Pond Shelter, at just over 11 miles. The shelter was a bit of a beauty, set on the top of a cliff overlooking Gentian Pond, though we stuck with our normal routine of tenting as opposed to using the shelter, and missed out on the view. At this site there were tenting platforms, always a bonus as far as I was concerned. My ability to find a sloping spot remained undiminished after nearly 2,000 miles of trying to find a flat spot.

We left Gentian Pond just after 7 a.m. with two impending targets. The first—the 1,900-mile marker—was upon us within the hour. The second was probably more significant, as we moved into Maine, our fourteenth and last state. Even though I'd allowed Katahdin to intrude upon my thoughts in recent weeks, it had still seemed remote and in the distant future. But we were now in Maine, and I couldn't ignore it. It felt good to add a dash of reality to my fantasy.

I also notched up another fall, number 36, catching my bent knee under my body. I'd been feeling particularly sore in my left knee just before I slipped. My instant thought was that I was going to break my leg, so far did I bend it. As I sat, defiantly calling out "36," I slowly released my leg to find that whatever it was that had been ailing me had stretched itself away. This was a bit of a novelty for me, in that I felt better after a fall than before. But I was happy to take it. I was aware that my falls were increasing with the difficulties we had encountered in New England, and I was desperately trying to avoid a bad fall that might jeopardize my hike. Being with a team gave me a sense of security, even though one false step could have finished any of us at any time.

    Maine was going to test all of us and we were excited at the challenge of our last state.

Chapter 24: Into Maine

Passing into Maine at mile 1904, we had a thrilling day's hike. We crossed Mount Carlo, Goose Eye Mountain (both East and North Peaks), as well as Fulling Mill Mountain South Peak.

Trillium had arranged for us to stay with one of her partner's relations, Geoff, for a couple of nights. We had arranged to meet Geoff at the end of our day, following a side trail for nearly three miles. He was going to meet us there and take us back to his cabin in the woods. I don't think any of us imagined how remote this pick-up spot was going to be. When we got there my heart sank, along, I'm sure, with the others'. At best, it seemed we would have a long wait. At worst, he wouldn't find us, so we'd have to backtrack three miles to rejoin the trail.

Trillium seemed to have the least doubt among us and she turned out to be right. To our wonder and amazement, Geoff drove up our deserted forest road only a few minutes after we had arrived. He greeted us all warmly, as if this was a journey he made every day, despite having no previous knowledge of the spot. He had agreed to slackpack us through the Mahoosuc Notch the following day, which meant that we had the luxury of only taking a daypack, then returning to his cabin that same evening. Given the reputation of Mahoosuc Notch as the toughest mile on the trail, this was a real bonus.

Geoff had a disorganized, though cozy, home, and he made us all feel very welcome following the long drive back. Lighterknot and I were on the floor, while Trillium and Tee Bird took the sofas. Geoff was not a hiker himself, though he had gleaned that hikers are generally ravenous, so he went out to get some food at a local restaurant. He returned with burgers and meatloaf meals for Lighterknot and me—both of which we happily demolished—while the girls contented themselves with something lighter.

The following morning, while Geoff drove us to the side trail that would eventually lead us back to the A.T., I noticed that clouds had formed over the mountains. They looked like a comforter thrown carelessly over the peaks. The sight augured well for the rest of the day, because there was a sparkling blue sky everywhere else, so we knew that the sun was steadily burning the comforter away.

Mahoosuc Notch is a collection of colossal boulders, making up a puzzle for hikers that is about a mile long. There were choices to be made as to whether to go over, go round, or even go under rocks, while we threaded our way through this deliciously chaotic mile. The white blazes painted on the rocks weren't just keeping us on track, they were showing us the way through the puzzle, with several right-angled arrows denoting a possible solution. We took our time, on many occasions stopping for a breather to reflect upon this crazy path. There was nowhere else on the trail that was anything like Mahoosuc Notch, and we became totally immersed in its intricacies, happily letting other, faster hikers pass us while we stopped for snacks. It was a lot of fun, taking us almost three hours as a team to finally get through.

Once we had negotiated that, there was an extensive climb up Mahoosuc Arm so that, by lunchtime, we had only done just over two miles of the trail. The sun had completed its job, and we were rewarded for our hard work—as so often in New England—by yet another great view at the top, with Old Speck ahead at the end of a ridge. We could also see what would turn out to be an endless climb down to Grafton Notch, a descent of 2,500 feet in nearly four miles.

As the afternoon progressed, I fell twice more—for the thirty-seventh, then the thirty-eighth time. The second time was fairly uneventful, and didn't hurt too much, though the first was one of my worst falls. I was making my way up a very steep, sheer rock face. I had just left the safety of a tree root that I'd been pulling myself up with to get to another one, when I felt my boots slip slightly on the rock. I thought I'd steadied myself, then made the fatal error of relaxing for an instant. I took off, sliding like a giraffe wearing socks, before falling about 15 to 20 feet, badly banging my hip as I went down.

As always, I defiantly shouted out the number of the fall as soon as I realized that I was neither bleeding nor dead. However, this call was accompanied by a grimace, as I felt the sharp pain. There never seemed to be much point in hanging around in these circumstances, so I got up and got on with it. Everything worked as before, though the hip hurt like blazes every other step.

My pace slowed quite a bit after my fall, making the climb down seem endless, while the temperature dropped and the wind increased. Eventually, at the end of a long, strenuous day and with the light starting to fail, we met Geoff on Maine 26 at Grafton Notch. He had clearly got to grips with the catering side of our endeavor, and took us for an excellent Chinese meal that hit the spot.

Geoff had to drop us off early at Grafton Notch the following morning. He needed to get to work, so we loaded our surplus stuff into bags, then left them at the back of his house, to be collected by the folks at The Cabin, our next stay, in Andover.

Once more carrying lighter packs, the hiking was easier. We made our way up and over the Baldpate Mountains—East and West. At over 3,500 feet, we were above the tree line, which always worked for me.

Slackpacking had become a practice that we were getting used to, and we were aware that many of our fellow hikers were doing the same thing. By now, Tee Bird had emerged as our booking agent. She had arranged for us to be met by Earl—or Bear—the proprietor of The Cabin at East B Hill Road, near Andover.

Bear and his wife, Honey—or Margie—had run The Cabin for 20 years. They were two of the most gracious people on the trail. Both in their 80s, they expected to be closing at the end of the 2014 season, for they were starting to feel their age. The highlight of the stay was dinner, served family style around an over-sized pine table, with Honey and Bear presiding at the top of the table, soaking up the stories and jokes of the hikers. The food was fresh and unlimited, with Bear pushing us all to eat more. We had wonderful evenings for each of the three nights that we stayed there, with friends old and new providing a changing cast of characters each night.

Breakfast was similarly unlimited. I had eight pancakes the next morning, along with eggs, sausage, and home fries that hardly touched the sides on the way down.

There was only room for five people in the cab of Bear's truck, while there were six of us to be transported back to the trail. We were traveling with four women, who I could only refer to as chatty, so I quickly jumped in the back, leaving Lighterknot and the ladies to travel in the cab.

As we were climbing a hill, the back of the truck fell open, and I had to rapidly grab packs and poles to stop them all falling out. Nobody noticed in the cab, as there was the constant drone of women talking, audible above the engine noise, as if it were a competitive sport. When Lighterknot got out, he was shaking his head and muttering, in his heavy southern drawl, "I should have sat in the back." For the rest of the day I could see him shaking his head from side to side as he walked ahead of me. It made me laugh, and still makes me laugh, whenever I think of it.

The configuration of the roads in this part of Maine limited the distance we could do from Andover to just a ten-mile day. Bear was there waiting for us by the time we reached South Arm Road. We had been delayed by both the climb up Moody Mountain and the resulting perilous climb down. It wasn't so much the distance we had to travel, it was more the slippery rocks we had to negotiate. Each of us remained fully engaged throughout the descent. We were very glad to see Bear's truck when we emerged at the bottom.

Our second dinner at The Cabin was a replica of the first, with a few new characters to spice up the conversation, one of whom turned out to be far more interesting than we thought at the time.

Bear and Honey had met many people over the years and welcomed everybody as if they were the most important guests ever to stay there. Several returned year in year out, and some would help with chores or the cooking. Hopper was a charming, pragmatic woman who had been a hiker for years. She was helping out for the week at The Cabin before resuming her hike.

This was far more civilized "work for stay" than the New Hampshire huts; she seemed genuinely pleased to be helping out. Her boyfriend, Bismarck, turned up on our second night. He was a quiet, thickly bearded guy, with a twinkle in his eye and an easy smile. They were a very together couple who seemed absorbed in hiking as a lifestyle and entirely self-contained.

It was consequently something of an eye-opener when I read on a social media posting in May 2015, that Bismarck had been considerably more than the sum of his apparent parts.

He had been the target of a number of law enforcement agencies, including the FBI, and had been arrested in Damascus, Virginia—the quintessential trail town—on charges of embezzling $8.7m from his previous employer, an Ohio-based Pepsi distributor. It turned out that the 53-year-old Bismarck had previously gone by the name of James T. Hammes, and this liberated, affable hiker had once been an accountant. His story had been featured on two fugitive TV shows: *America's Most Wanted* and CNBC's *American Greed*. He was accused, over about an 11-year period, of taking the funds through a number of banking transfers while in his role as the financial controller for the distributor.

I've read that he pleaded guilty and, the last I heard, he was awaiting sentencing. All I know is that he was an affable man to me, though his emerging story militated against everything I'd learned about people on the trail. I'm sure it was far worse for him, but, for me, I was sad to read of his demise.

The third slackpack out of Bear and Honey's was a more respectable 13 miles, with Bear predicting that we would finish at 5 o'clock. The old boy certainly knew his stuff, because I emerged at Maine 17 at precisely 4:59 p.m., watching him grinning at me in his logistical triumph. Even from this parking area there was another stupendous view to add to my Maine collection.

Back at The Cabin for our last evening, I was reacquainted with two of the Rocky Pizza Challenge participants, Hawkeye and Buchanan. It was the first time I had seen either of them since Tennessee. We all marveled at how our paths, and others, had intersected over the last half year. That theme returned to me every time I ran into an old friend. Our mutual respect was based upon the fact that, whatever difficulties we had experienced, we had both made it to the same place and at the same time. For me, that was a strong validation of my newly acquired status as a hiker.

We spent three nights at The Cabin, slackpacking each day. Our booking agent, Tee Bird, had made arrangements to move on to Rangely, where we were going to stay with Shane and Stacey, at the Farmhouse. Having both looked after ourselves for nearly 2,000 miles, Lighterknot and I were perfectly content to pass over logistical arrangements to Tee Bird and, to a lesser extent, Trillium. I'm not sure if this speaks more of our *laissez-faire* attitude, or of the innate laziness of men; I suspect the latter.

The hike that day was a 13-miler, with fairly easy topography that was welcome, given that the next few days looked like a heart-stopping frenetic roller coaster. A quiet day's hike from time to time was always helpful between the mountains.

The Farmhouse was another sprawling hostel that gave us proper beds and a truly communal spirit. You could lap the building, in and out of bedrooms and sitting rooms on a continuous loop. Stacey ran the place with a charmingly relaxed demeanor, while Shane drove us into town and slackpacked us.

Rangely was a small town, with a couple of excellent restaurants that seemed to welcome hikers. It was good to meet up with Yeti Legs and Tumbles once more, as they had deliberately slowed down to enjoy every last day in the woods. These two guys personified everything I learned about generations younger than my own. They were optimistic, caring, and living perfectly in the moment. Once the hike was over, Yeti Legs decided to follow the same profession as Tumbles, a nurse. There were several hundreds of men and women on the trail, many of whom I met, developing a similar perspective. I'm glad that I ran into these two. I could cite others, but these two were extra-special people.

Shane and Stacey had only recently established themselves at the Farmhouse, yet I could instantly see that Shane was going to be, at the very least, a future mayor of the town. He knew everybody, having a friendly word for all as he passed them. Sometimes you run into people who have an overload of charisma and they seem destined for bigger things. I felt strongly that Shane was such a man.

Chapter 25: More mountains

I've often wondered if my reflections on places in which we stayed were colored by the type of hikes that we had from them. Every day out of the Farmhouse led us to a new, spectacular adventure that strengthened our legs and resolve equally. Returning each night, we felt exhausted, but satisfied with our efforts.

Our first hike out, which started on a crisp, clear day, took us up nearly 2,500 feet to the top of Saddleback Mountain. Well before we reached the summit, the clouds dropped down to visit us, so visibility was only about 50 feet. While this is fine for walking, it is fairly useless when it comes to sightseeing. We missed some special views, though we knew they were out there. I know that to be the case as, an hour later, we were on Saddleback Junior, and the clouds had pushed off for the day, giving us another magnificent Maine panorama.

This was one of those above-the-treeline days that resonated with me. Photos I had seen of Maine prior to starting  the trail had seemed so out of reach, being more than 2,000 miles in my future. But here I was, in a previously imagined place that was exponentially more exciting than even I had contemplated. Sharing this with Lighterknot, Tee Bird, and Trillium was an unexpected bonus of hiking in a group; I would have hated to have seen all of this alone.

The next day out of the Farmhouse led us up and over Lone Mountain, then along a nearly-seven-mile ridge that was interrupted by a lively trek up Spaulding Mountain. From Spaulding, on this sparkling, clear day, we could see across to the ski slope on Sugarloaf. A ski slope with no snow seemed incongruous to me on this unseasonably warm day. A sharp descent to a forest road left us with a mile-and-a-half walk back to meet Shane at Caribou Valley Road, because he was unable to drive all the way up the forest road to meet us.

It was around this time that I worked out our options for a finishing date by looking at the mileage we could realistically do in the coming weeks. We all sat around and decided on September 29. It was a practical result that finally squashed any chance I had entertained of returning home in time for Diane's birthday. Having this goal gave me closure on that notion, focusing me more clearly on these last miles. I don't think I had ever fully understood the concept of achievable, realistic goals prior to this hike, and I checked this off as one more lesson learned.

The plan for the following day—worked out again by Tee Bird—was that we would move our traveling circus on to the Stratton Motel and Hostel. Sue, who was the owner of our new digs, and Shane, passed on hikers like a baton in a relay race. Such an arrangement suited our team perfectly.

We started this third day very early, on a bitterly cold morning. We were driven back to the trail via Stratton, dropping our excess baggage at Sue's hostel before heading back to where we had left off the day before.

On the way, we took a road known locally as Moose Alley, due to the frequent altercations that occurred between moose and car. Some moose can grow to 1,200 pounds and possess negligible road skills, so these meetings can often go badly for the car. Seeing a moose on the trail, as we had done previously, was a big deal. However, even seeing one on the road is a sight to behold. Suddenly, ahead of us, two magnificent beasts—one male, one female—emerged from the woods and bolted across the road. Luckily, the car ahead managed to avoid them comfortably, and we had a few seconds to watch open-mouthed as they plunged back into the forest. This stuff just didn't get old, nor should it.

As usual, we started with a hefty ascent, up from Caribou Valley Road, to South and North Crocker Mountains. It was a perilous 2,000-foot climb, some of which was over very exposed rocks in high winds. Once over the two peaks, though, there was a very comfortable downhill all the way back to the main road. There, we were lucky enough to run into a couple of previous thru-hikers, who drove us all to the hostel in Stratton. Getting into a car and *not* seeing the driver reach for the window control as the odor hit him squarely in the face was a pleasant change.

While the four of us were hiking as a team, we had been joined intermittently by a quirky, but constantly affable young man named Karate Kid. He was far quicker and younger than us, but seemed to enjoy our company. He was also a lot of fun to be around. Karate Kid seemed to accept that when somebody had to squeeze into an uncomfortable position in a car, or be left to brave the cold in the back of a truck, then he would smilingly go ahead and be that somebody.

At the hostel, Lighterknot, Karate Kid, and I headed straight to the inn next door, Wolf Inn. Here we discovered the massive and succulent Wolf Burger, hopefully named after the inn, not the contents. My carbohydrate overdose left me crashed out contentedly on my bunk for a couple of hours, with thoughts of the upcoming Bigelow Mountains sending me off to sleep.

I've already referred to a few previous days as my best day's hiking, yet our day in the Bigelows was another time that eclipsed everything that had come before.

We set off on another "slackpacking opportunity," as Tee Bird would refer to them, and had planned for a 17-mile day. There were three peaks above 3,500 feet, with the easier Little Bigelow Mountain thrown in as a bonus. After a couple of hours, we came to the deceptively steep South Horn. In the guide, it had looked a breeze, but it turned out to be steeper than anything we had seen in Maine, albeit over a relatively short distance.

The sun was out and, while it was chilly, our exertions allowed us to remain warm all day, especially with the next two Bigelow Mountain peaks—West Peak and Avery Peak. These two epitomized hiking in Maine for me. They were exposed and challenging, but never felt too onerous. I was drawn in by the beauty all around, along with the sense of adventure that this high ridge imbued within me. When we reached the top of Avery Peak, the wind was kicking up all around us and it compounded the adventure.

Sue met us at East Flagstaff Road, and we returned to the motel in perfect time for another Wolf Burger at the Wolf Inn. With so many calories burned during the day, this one hardly touched the sides on the way down. Sometimes, when you hit upon a winner, why would you look at the rest of the menu? I have a funny feeling that one of my ex-wives once said that to me, though I don't believe she was referring to burgers at the time.

By contrast with the day before, the following morning opened dark and brooding. Rain was expected, and eventually fell during the morning, then into the early afternoon. We were back to our full packs. Even though it took a while to readjust to our normal burden, we all managed well, because we were able to put in another 16-plus-mile day. There were no extended climbs; we didn't even go above 2000 feet, with Roundtop the only distinguishable mountain.

Slackpacking had certainly made the days easier. However, the psychological impact of carrying a full pack, for me, was to appreciate rest when I took it, and camp when I reached it. I felt that we had become a little soft out of the woods, and, while I sat quietly with Lighterknot over dinner, we both agreed that it was good to be back in our tents for the night. There was a stillness and serenity to sleeping in a tent that I only noticed I was missing when I'd been away from it for some time. I think the gradually draining light and lengthening shadows also played into the feeling on that evening.

We were camped at Pierce Pond Lean-to, all of us managing to find decent tent sites, despite the protruding roots all over the ground. It was tough enough during the day coping with roots, so the fact that they continued to bug us once we had stopped seemed somehow unfair to me.

The next day, we had planned a relatively low mileage day, having camped less than four miles short of the Kennebec River. The river was about 150 yards wide, and the A.T.C. provided a ferryman who paddled hikers across in his canoe, two at a time. This was quite possibly the world's most repetitive, yet most beautiful, job.

We got there on another delicious day, with an early morning mist hovering over the water to greet us. Within five minutes the mist had been totally burned off by the sun. We could see our ride heading our way. Tee Bird and Lighterknot went first, while Trillium and I followed a few minutes later.

"Hillbilly" Dave Corrigan was our ferryman. He proceeded to tell us about the river and the ferry, clearly proud of his part in every hiker's epic journey. He knew his stuff, being particularly amusing when he talked of the times he had intervened to save purists who were determined to ford the river. There are some who insist that the hike isn't complete unless you ford the river and ignore the canoe. All I can say to that is that the Catholic Church seems to think I'm still married to my first wife. I can prove that I divorced her in 1986, and that I have since married twice more. Get over yourselves, and let others move on, even if you don't want to.

    Once across, we took our planned short detour to the post office in Caratunk, where Tee Bird was picking up a restock package from her husband. Trillium had a package delivered by her partner to a local hotel, so we called for a shuttle. We were soon picked up, then whisked to a very pretty hotel. Here, we were able to restock; in my case, this meant more Snickers and peanut butter. Unfortunately, the hotel wasn't able to provide hot meals—other than frozen pizza or burgers—so the owner considerately drove us to the Kennebec River Pub & Brewery.

    This was one of those build-your-own-burger places. Despite a basic price of about $8 for a bun and a half-pound patty, Karate Kid and I both ended up with massive $20 superburgers. These included lettuce, tomato, onion, mayo, several cheeses, bacon, and a fried egg, as well as an extra half-pound slab of meat. Had I been physically able to add anything else to this colossal meal, I undoubtedly would have done so. I'd like to say that I am ashamed of such an outrageous display of gluttony, but I'm afraid I can't. In fact, I followed my burger by demolishing a brownie with cream and ice cream, then washed it all down with two beers. I may have borne a striking resemblance to a starving refugee, but I wasn't going down without a fight.

We persuaded the guy who ran the noon shuttle back to the trail to delay it for "a few minutes." We eventually left for the trailhead, stuffed, and in something of a calorific stupor, by 1:15.

Amazingly, as I waddled up the trail, I ran into Bassman, about to start a section hike heading south. He was the guy I had hiked with many hundreds of miles before, and who had later helped me run around to get some errands done in Connecticut. I didn't have time to chat, because the team had already moved ahead, but it was great to see him again.

We hiked another six miles to get to the Pleasant Pond Lean-to, setting up some way back in the woods. One of the youngsters at the shelter bravely dove into the pond to cool off. As I understood the temperature in these ponds to be about 40 degrees Fahrenheit, I could only shake my head, concluding that we were all young and immortal once.

Leaving Pleasant Pond the following morning, we had a steady hike up Pleasant Pond Mountain, following which we were treated to a benign descent over several miles that eventually moved back uphill over Moxie Bald Mountain, leading us ultimately to Moxie Bald Lean-to. It seems that when naming their shelters, Maine decided to forgo originality, simply naming them after the nearest topographical feature. We loved this latter site, as we were all able to tent close to, and in sight of, the magnificent pond, unsurprisingly named Moxie Pond.

The night was cold, and I heard the haunting, plaintive cries of loons, on and around the pond. These birds had such a distinctive call. It was an unexpected bonus of Maine that I'd heard before, though never so loud as on this night. Our proximity to the pond seemed to amplify the sound, which filled my tent as I drifted off to sleep.

When I woke before dawn, the sun was still below the horizon, so I set up my breakfast on the rocks right next to the water. I was rewarded by the sun easing dramatically and dazzlingly into the new day. There was complete silence, with a beaver messing about in the water less than 20 feet from me. The others joined me, and we soaked up the sun, somewhat reluctant to get on our way while we were slowly warming.

Our original plan for the next two days was to complete the 18-mile journey into Monson. We intended to stealth-camp about four miles short of Monson, then complete the trip early on Saturday morning.

The hike, for the most part, was unremarkable. There were no mountains to scale, and it was a generally easy walk in the woods. We just had rocks and those darn roots to watch out for. What made this day memorable, though, was the fact that there were two fairly wide rivers to ford that demanded all our attention.

The first was the most fun, as the only way to do it was to wade across, removing boots and socks, then rolling up our pant legs. There was a rope suspended across the river to help us. However, the water was fairly shallow and we used the rope more to steady ourselves than to prevent being swept away. With the water in Maine now devastatingly cold, each step was accompanied by either a curse or a gasp on my part. By the time I got to the other side, I could neither feel my feet nor conjure up further expletives to adequately express myself. Fortunately, nobody fell in, and the second crossing was completed with boots on. This incorporated rock-hopping and eventually balancing precariously while we walked along a fallen tree. Lighterknot led the way on this one. He found the best route while the rest of us were stranded in the middle, quietly regretting keeping our boots on.

We didn't need to stealth-camp that night. A brand new hostel and campsite had opened only three miles from Monson, just off the trail, so we gave it a shot. A former thru-hiker, Phil, had built a terrific compact camp. There were private and semi-private cabins, as well as flat tent sites in an area he had cut out in the woods. The cabins were beautifully constructed, though we stayed in our tents to save money. Phil even lent us his truck to go into Monson for dinner.

With less than four miles to go that Saturday morning, we quickly got to Maine 15. There, we were picked up by a shuttle from Shaw's, Monson's main hostel. Another artery-clogging breakfast at Pete's Place was dispatched, then the day was spent showering and washing clothes for the upcoming 100-Mile Wilderness.

While we were in Pete's Place, I happened to mention to one of the owners—neither of whom were named Pete—that I was looking for a groundsheet. I told her that the floor of my tent had developed a few small holes, and that I was keen to avoid any rising dampness or creepy crawlies joining me in the middle of the night. She told me that there was an outfitter in a nearby town, some 15 miles away, and that I was welcome to borrow her car if I'd like. The generosity of complete strangers remained a wonder to me, but I was soon driving a car for the first time in half a year. It felt strangely alien, and I can't say that I enjoyed the experience, though I certainly appreciated the gesture.

Chapter 26: Monson and slackpacking

The 100-Mile Wilderness was neither precisely 100 miles, nor was it actually a wilderness. However, this last stretch, taking us to within spitting distance of Mount Katahdin, had been on my mind for several days, and was also the place I believed that I'd be most tested. We had been successfully slackpacking for a few weeks, resupplying regularly, but now we knew that full packs would be needed. We would also have to carry herculean amounts of food for this 100-mile stint.

At least, that's what we had been told.

Shaw's Hiker Hostel was perfectly situated. It was not only a comfortable stop prior to tackling the wilderness but was also a wonderful meeting place for those of us on the verge of a fantastic achievement. There was a noticeable buzz about the place when we pitched up. I was lucky enough to snag a room with two beds, though the second bed remained unoccupied throughout my stay, giving me my preferred privacy. The spare bed became a repository for all my junk. Everything about Shaw's was done with the hiker in mind. There was Wi-Fi, washing facilities (for both clothes and bodies), decent beds, and clean sheets. Add to this a blow-out breakfast and you can see why Shaw's checked all the boxes.

We needed to leave earlier than most each morning, so our team stuck with Pete's Place for breakfast. Our excellent decision rewarded us with more than enough calories for our day. The fact that there was also a great pub a short walk away from Shaw's made it the perfect storm for our last shot at civilization before the end of our hike.

Tee Bird was still our booking agent for slackpacking. She had heard from a couple of female thru-hikers, Smasher and Spirit, that there was a man in town named Buddy who was a shuttle driver. Buddy could be persuaded, for a fee, to slackpack us for about 45 miles of the 100-Mile Wilderness. This would take care of the main mountains, and get us well on our way to Katahdin. In the end, it was Trillium who did the deal with Buddy. Once it was done, we were able to look forward to the next few evenings in Monson.

The first day, Sunday, Buddy drove us out to Long Pond Stream. In trail miles, it was just over 14 miles north of Monson. As luck would have it, this meant that we had an immediate ford to negotiate, Little Wilson Stream. Inevitably, I was the only one who didn't quite make it across, managing to dunk my boot into the stream, with the resulting *squelch* keeping me company for the rest of the day.

Once that incident had passed we had a fairly uneventful hike, with the expected rain not materializing as strongly as the forecast had indicated. We got back to Maine 15, and Shaw's, with only minimal drying out required.

About 100 yards before we reached the road, as we passed out of the forest, we came across a sign for NOBOs that made us smile.

Appalachian Trail
Caution
There are no places to obtain supplies or get help until Abol Bridge 100 miles north. Do not attempt this section unless you have a minimum of 10 days supplies and are fully equipped. This is the longest wilderness section of the entire AT and its difficulty should not be underestimated.
Good Hiking! MATC

I particularly warmed to the gloom-and-doom warning followed by the rather jolly note of encouragement, emphasized by an exclamation point.

Once dry, we headed down to the local pub, forming an ever-larger table with about ten other excited hikers joining us to share experiences. We were all aware that the end was so close, and, on this evening, it hit me harder than I let on to my team.

Back in my room, I allowed myself the luxury of imagining that I was at home once more. I thought about the changes that I knew had taken place since I had stepped out of my marriage, almost exactly six months previously.

Diane had been caring for her folks more and more, and I knew that she had now set an expectation of her presence on their part. She would leave home at about 6:30 in the morning, then return three hours later. At any time between 2:30 and 3:30 p.m. she would go back to them. Finally, she would get back to our home by about 6:30 or 7 p.m. I knew this to be the case, because she had often recounted these hours to me. I could only see my return through the prism of those hours.

While I wasn't sure how this would work out, it was clear to me that I would be stepping back into the marriage—though only part of the way back. I would be spending plenty of time alone, and would have to find things to do on my own. Before you think that this is perhaps the way most marriages should be run—and I have friends who mentioned that to me—imagine what this actually means. Diane would, by and large, be unavailable for many, if any, otherwise shared experiences during the day and many evenings. I knew I'd be making my own schedule, as if still single. Given my past proclivities, this was a state of affairs that I felt would be healthier to avoid. I knew that it was inevitable that we'd be spending less time as a couple. That bothered me. Mind you, I also knew that Diane's presence in her folks' lives had become central to their day. They had survived, prospered even, because of her devotion. If I had tried to pressure her to leave some time for the two of us, I think it would have laid the groundwork for a resentment that would be insoluble should her parents' health deteriorate as a result.

That night, while I lay there in the dark, with the occasional thud and muffled laughter coming from one part of the house or another, with my hopes soon to be fulfilled on the trail, I knew that I'd be returning to a less than complete marriage. Such a reflection led me to weigh these competing emotions, ultimately settling upon a decision regarding my marriage that, in previous years, I would have been unlikely to make.

I have already mentioned my less-than-strict adherence to my marriage vows in the past, so my record was spotty in this regard, to say the least. However, my marriage to Diane had been so unexpected, so wonderful, and her impact upon me so beneficial, that the vows that we had made to one another in the Turks and Caicos islands seven years before now came home to me in the framework of this new reality. Despite an unknown future, despite a need for her company and her attention, I decided that night that I would not only keep those vows but I would also try to live my life as fully as possible, and wait for her to rejoin me in our marriage. I may have been the one who walked away into the woods, but she had also helped upend the marriage by her understandable commitment to her parents.

I've learned over the years that no condition is permanent. I also knew that, eventually, we would be a couple again. I could wait. I have the patience, but I'm glad I went through another conversation in my head that, like the many others before it on the trail, I really needed to have before I finally got home. Thus resolved, I allowed myself to drop off to sleep.

Having done the first 15 or so miles of the Wilderness, Buddy returned to the same spot the following morning. He pointed us north this time, giving us a slightly longer hike that would end at Katahdin Iron Works Road.

It was a great day, spoiled by one daft slip on my part.

Rain had continued through the night, but the forecast told us, correctly, that it was expected to blow through after about 9 a.m. The rain gave way to bright sunshine, with a breeze that kept us cool. The guide promised plenty of ups and downs, with lots of opportunities to keep warm as we pushed uphill. I've heard these ups and downs referred to as PUDS—pointless ups and downs—although they never seemed pointless to me. The elevation changes were tough throughout the entire trail, but it would have been boring as hell without them. I cursed as much as anybody when I could see the descending path rising ahead. That said, I wouldn't have changed a single one of them.

With the rain replaced by an intermittently clear blue sky, it was a terrific day for views. The spectacular lakes, or ponds, continued to draw the eye, with the view from Barren Ledges on Barren Mountain being one that burned itself on my retina forever. Maine and New Hampshire, more than any other states, proved the inadequacy of cameras on the A.T., so I always tried to store these great days in my brain, pulling them out from time to time to revisit them. The colors may have faded, but they still look far better than they do on a 6" by 4" photograph.

We had also experienced a few cold nights, with the impact upon the foliage startling. Back at these slightly higher elevations, we were able to see what looked like a warm-up for Monet, as he dabbed orange, yellow, and even pink paint on the green canvas below. We first noticed this crossing Third Mountain, as the valley opened up in front of us. The rest of the week saw the old boy get into his stride, with explosions of color all around as we passed through.

This day turned out to be excellent preparation for our legs, as, with Katahdin coming up, any extra help in the leg department was going to be welcome. We were all as strong as oxen by this time, but Katahdin looked like Mount Doom in the guide. It loomed over us as we drew closer. I think I now know how Frodo must have felt.

I had just been speaking with another thru-hiker—my team having hiked on—when I turned to hurry after them. I slipped on a large, wet tree trunk that was across my path. I flipped in the air for my forty-fifth, and what turned out to be my most dramatic, fall of the trip. As I came down, in that slow motion way that we sometimes experience, I was aware of a rock to my left. I quickly flinched at a potential collision between skull and rock. Luckily, my head missed the rock, but I ended up wedged, literally, between a rock and a hard place, in this case, the log.

It was excruciatingly painful, but my first thought was that my phone had been in my back pocket. Helpless, I had to be pulled from my trap, slowly getting back to my feet. There was a considerable amount of blood coming from both arms, though I was relieved that nothing had been broken. My diagnosis turned out to be slightly premature, as I discovered on pulling my phone from my pocket. The impact had shattered the glass and bent the frame of the phone. Astonishingly, it continued to operate as both a phone and a camera until the end. With less than 100 miles to go, it seemed appropriate that my phone should share some of my battering.

In what had been something of a hallmark of the trip, I had no real alternative other than to carry on, so I did just that. I winced from time to time, but was relieved that not only was I not dead but I was also able to walk and make a phone call. Seeing positives in negatives was another benefit from this hike. I defy anybody who has hiked the Appalachian Trail not to have discovered this skill.

Buddy had judged our woefully slow walking pace perfectly. He was there to meet us as we emerged, tired from going over five mountains, but elated to have wiped out another 15 miles of the wilderness. The ride back to Monson was an hour this time, with another trip to the pub as our reward.

Back at Katahdin Iron Works Road the following morning, with my left leg aching sporadically, we had planned another 15-miler that took us over White Cap, the last high mountain before Katahdin. It was to be our second-from-last day slackpacking, and we appreciated our lighter packs once more. While White Cap was the highest we had climbed since the Bigelows, we were crossing a ridge of peaks all day long.

We emerged at West Branch Ponds Road, a full two-hour drive back to Monson, including an 18-mile bumpety-bump along a dirt road used by logging trucks. I'm not the finest of travelers at the best of times, so this drive had me feeling a little under the weather by the time we arrived in Monson. Of course, I wasn't so under the weather as to avoid my last calorific overdose.

That night, our last in Monson, I met up again with Sherpa. I had originally bumped into him just before the Smokies, and had only seen him once since then. Two of the fearless young women, Bluebird and Simba, were also there. They both hugged me excitedly, as I did them. Simba seemed shocked by my reduced physique and wasn't afraid to tell me how awful I looked—bless her. For my part, I was delighted to see that virtually all the young women I had met on this trail had made it to here and beyond. I'd seen entries in the shelter logs that confirmed that Tigger, Stylze, Hawkeye, and Twist had passed through. Of course, I had worried about Stardust as well. Now that Simba and Bluebird were nearing the end, I felt a kind of paternal relief. They must have really made their folks proud.

There was also a mother and daughter combination at Monson—Bad Camel and Popeye. They had started the hike as a family, with Bad Camel's husband accompanying them. Unfortunately, he had injured himself and needed to quit the trail. Somewhat uncharitably, he suggested that they wouldn't survive without him. Hmm. If there is anything that today's woman will respond to, it is today's man telling her that she can't survive without him. Popeye—the daughter—had a glint in her eye as she told this story over dinner that night. Few people had a better motive for getting their picture taken on top of Mount Katahdin than these two wonderful women. My guess is that they will be sharing their story for many years to come. Silly man, Mr. Camel.

We were now almost out of slackpacking opportunities, though one more remained. Our uncomfortable drive of the previous evening was retraced, before Buddy waved us off. He was staying in the area for a bit of fishing, before meeting us later at Jo-Mary Road. We would be at mile 2,130, where he would then hand over the remainder of our packs.

It turned out to be an easy day's hiking, with the gorgeous Crawford Pond an exquisitely tranquil highlight. We could see more of the developing colors as we looked across the lake to the gentler hills ahead.

Leaving Buddy and our link to Monson behind, we assumed our full packs once more. As the light was beginning to fade, we headed a mile or so into the woods. The sun had almost gone when I saw an opening, just off the path. I found a spot for a couple of tents for me and Lighterknot, while the women moved deeper into the forest to set up about 30 yards from us. As before, it was great to be back in the woods. I sat on a log preparing my pasta, with only the twittering nuthatches as company; it was very calming, and I felt at home again.

Chapter 27: Last miles

We were now on the final few days. A glance at the guide showed that these last 55 miles were fairly flat, apart, of course, for the devastating steepness that indicated our goal. We had tried to spot Katahdin from previous peaks, and had guessed where it might be, though we had never been sure. The following morning provided us with a view that defied any doubts.

It was a searingly bright and blue day as we pitched up to the edge of Pemadumcook Lake, with the track passing within feet of the water. This opened up an unobstructed view of Katahdin to our left, still nearly 50 miles of walking away from us. It is hard to overstate our excitement, and we posed for pictures with one another as if to confirm that the end was clearly in reach. The four of us were joined by another few hikers. Everybody quieted down as the reality of our imminent success gripped us. The fact that our target seemed to be increasing in size as we got closer didn't appear to put any of us off. We sped on to Nahmakanta Lake with adrenalin infusing each step.

The flat terrain allowed us to reach this beautiful lake earlier than usual and, having set up camp a few feet back into the woods, we hung out on the stones beside the lake, enjoying the afternoon sun as it dropped slowly out of sight to the west. I was mesmerized by the peace of the place. I sat for over an hour on a rock thinking about my time on the trail, as well as my hopes for my return to Diane.

My inner thoughts concerning my marriage a few nights previously had allowed me some peace, so I could only look forward with positivity. I knew the challenges were there, and I knew I'd still have my moments of doubt. On the plus side, I also knew that I'd found my person, as Diane often referred to me. Having put a lot of groundwork into finding the right one, I certainly didn't want to start the interview process again.

Nahmakanta turned out to be one of my favorite campsites, because all doubt was now extinguished, at least in my mind. We were going to finish, as a team. There were no major hurdles in front of us, other than Katahdin, of course. All I expected out of the hike was that I'd get a shot at climbing

Katahdin, and we would all be doing this, together, in a few days' time.

As we left Nahmakanta the following morning, the path took us out of the woods for about 200 yards, leading us along the beach around the lake for that short distance. I savored this unexpected treat before a white blaze took us back into the woods, where we stayed for most of the day. On the way, we passed several lakes, then stumbled upon a couple of moose. It was a mother and her calf. Sadly, I wasn't able to grab my camera in time to record these two, suddenly emerging from the bushes about 25 yards ahead of us. We watched, open-mouthed in my case, as they sauntered back into the woods to continue their assault on the limitless leaves. Seeing the majesty of such animals in their own, very comfortable environment, is humbling and reduces humans to awestruck onlookers. Having started my hike with the view that any animal encounters would have to be endured, I was now eagerly experiencing them as the very essence of excitement on the trail.

We were lucky that evening to find almost as great a spot as Nahmakanta, setting up at Rainbow Spring campsite, a little further back into the woods, but with an easy stroll to the lake. Soon, we were joined by about a dozen others. We all gathered to watch the sun go down from the small opening by the lake, scattered around on the rocks, with everybody lost in his or her own thoughts.

The following morning, I got there early, with nobody for company. I filmed as the sun pulled itself up to light the trees on the opposite bank. I had been appreciating my light show alone, but was glad to see Lighterknot as he joined me for breakfast. We sat there in companionable silence, with both our destination and home beckoning in our immediate futures.

It was now Saturday morning. We were all feeling the anticipation of Monday's climb, though we were growing concerned about the weather forecast. We had been appreciating the beauty of the past few weeks, but were now ready to go home. We were also keenly aware that Monday was forecast to let us down, with a 50 percent chance of rain. It was especially disappointing, since we had been treated to cloudless weather for most of the week. Indeed, both Saturday and Sunday were expected to continue in this vein.

The walk out of the wilderness, to the deeply unattractive Abol Bridge, was easy and mainly flat. However, a wonderful trip across Rainbow Ledges gave us another glorious shot of our goal. Much to our later amusement, Tee Bird and I spent the previous ten minutes believing that we had identified

Katahdin, a short distance further back. A few minutes later we realized that we had been looking in precisely the wrong direction. The real thing, when we saw it, couldn't be mistaken.

I'm not sure if it was the anticipation of the finish, or the accumulative effect of my 45 falls, but I was struggling on what should have been an easy day. When I mentioned this to Lighterknot, he felt exactly the same, so we presumed it to be the former. By this time we both felt very emotional, and our inner turmoil appeared to be having a detrimental effect upon our physical well-being. These feelings may seem silly to some of you, but they were real—and disconcerting—when they hit us.

To do what the two of us were doing required a lot of commitment, and not all of it was from us. Our families had endured our hikes from a distance, worried more than us, and they were equally looking forward to our return. I think we may have relaxed a little in anticipation of home, then found that the hiking became tougher as a result. Whatever it was, we descended from the beautiful Rainbow Ledges and were finally out of the 100-Mile Wilderness. The fact that we had slackpacked for half of the wilderness didn't bother me a jot. I would highly recommend others to do the same.

The only real attraction of Abol Bridge—apart from a beautiful shot of Katahdin from the bridge itself—is the fact that there is a campsite and a restaurant. We set up at the designated site, next to a wide river, within 100 yards of the restaurant. It was a great spot. Lighterknot and I demolished burgers for both lunch and dinner. With only one more evening before we climbed to our intended destiny, we weren't going to waste one of the last opportunities to eat disgracefully.

I had left it too late to take advantage of the shower that evening, so hurried into it at 5:30 the following morning. Unfortunately, once I had stripped naked, I was completely unable to make my chosen shower work. Gathering up my clothes, soap and towel, I darted across the room to the other shower before failing miserably to get any action from that one as well. I stood there, somewhat bemused as to what I had done wrong. Then, as with every fall, I just got on with it. I shrugged, pulled my filthy clothes back on to my filthy body, then returned to pack my tent. There was simply nothing I could do about it. Consequently, my trip up Katahdin was going to take place with the added weight of several days' worth of accumulated sweat and grime, with a commensurately filthy shirt.

Having started my trip six months previously with a selfie as a defense mechanism, I was ending it with a shrug for the same purpose. I presumed that was progress of a sort.

The traditional camping site for the night before the climb is in Baxter State Park, at the Katahdin Stream Campground. With just a flat ten miles to go from Abol Bridge, we took our time, even detouring to another pond, where we had a stupendous view of our goal. We were sitting on rocking chairs at the Daicey Pond visitor center, allowing ourselves to be intimidated by the brooding silence of Katahdin. I'm not sure how the others were feeling, but I was trying to stay calm and in the moment.

Arriving at the campground, there was a palpable excitement around us. Hikers were on their way down from that day's ascent. We greeted them as enthusiastically as heroes returning from combat. Everybody was high-fiving as they passed by, celebrating their epic achievement. By now, we all had a huge mutual respect. We were delighted to see our fellow hikers achieving what we were hoping to match in 24 hours' time. Then, it would be our turn, but this was their time.

Trillium's partner, Jon, had arranged a lean-to for the two of them. It was a mini-shelter that was bookable for a fee. Lighterknot had been met by his wife, Deb, and his mother, the indomitable Mama Jean. They were going into Millinocket for the night. Trillium and Jon graciously allowed Tee Bird and me to pitch our tents outside their lean-to. We were in a great position to greet and talk to the hikers as they returned with their stories of the day's climb. Unfortunately, just as dusk was upon us, a ranger came by to tell us that we weren't allowed to camp there. Even though we were in nobody's way, we had to move about 20 yards farther down. For that privilege, we were also charged $15 each to camp in this new spot. Despite getting particularly British on him, he wasn't to be moved. I had to accept the inevitable, so I dragged my already-erected tent to a new site. I was not happy.

Earlier, the same ranger had taken my registration to climb the mountain. He recorded me as the 699th successful thru-hiker of the year. While I liked the concept of being a successful thru-hiker, it felt a bit premature to me. He told us that between 3,000 and 4,000 hikers had started in Georgia, though numbers weren't finalized. It eventually transpired that there were an estimated 2,500 starters from Georgia in 2014, of which 653 completed their hike, while the SOBOs had 242 starters, with 76 climbing the scrubby little track that finished at Springer.

I could not have been more delighted that I had chosen to start at Springer. I felt strongly, as I still do, that the Katahdin finish was the icing on a very substantial cake. I would find this to be true the following morning, though I felt it strongly even before I started my final climb.

That night, I was unable to sleep too much, and sat up in my tent to contemplate what I was about to achieve. Funnily enough, one of the things that mattered to me most in those moments was the fact that my son, Rob, was going to accept my trail name, Mighty Blue. He had insisted, not unreasonably, that I couldn't claim to be mighty before I'd actually taken a step. He had already started calling me "Almost Mighty Blue" for a couple of weeks, so I knew that I was on the right track. His acceptance of my name was suddenly dreadfully important to me.

I also thought of what I was going to do when I returned to Florida. I had the luxurious feeling of not knowing, and being entirely open to anything that might come my way. That said, my return to Florida panned out in totally unexpected ways that I'm glad I didn't know that night.

Above all, of course, I was anticipating my return to Diane, then getting on with our lives. Stepping outside of your marriage, albeit with your partner's blessing and support, is a strange thing to happen in a strong marriage. I will always be grateful for her buy-in to my adventure. Whatever challenges we were going to face in the coming months and years could only be addressed once I was home. For now, all I could think about was seeing her lovely face.

My Appalachian Trial II: Creaking Geezer, Hidden Flagon

Chapter 28: Katahdin and beyond

Katahdin had always been our goal and had loomed at the end of my guidebook as a monumental climb that would bring to bear everything I had learned, as both a hiker and as a climber. Somehow, it seemed so fitting that we would finish with one last effort that would exceed all those that came before. Those previous miles were our preparation for this last trial.

Katahdin was named by the Penobscot Indians. The name means "The Greatest Mountain," a more-than-apt representation of its role in the lives of all A.T. thru-hikers. It is steep and formed from a granite intrusion that dwarfs everything around it for miles. In the 1930s, Governor Percival Baxter protected the area around the mountain, establishing Baxter State Park in the process. I'm not entirely sure how much protection the mountain needs, as it is part of some of the oldest mountains in the world. However, protection it gets, and that has led to some harsh words between hikers at the end of their journey and state park rangers.

It seems that the rangers object to the celebrations that erupt at the end of the hike as the famous brown sign is reached. Alcohol and dope are commonly cited as the drugs of choice. The proximity of families to these apparently abhorrent practices seems to inflame the passions of officials more than they really should. Surely, some form of release is understandable when hikers reach a goal that hasn't just been six months in the making. More often than not, it is the culmination of a long-held dream. A slug or a toke doesn't seem, to me, to be entirely out of order.

That said, all hikers should realize—if they haven't already over the previous 2,185 miles—that we are lucky to have the opportunity to take advantage of the American Park system, one of the finest in the world. Daft behavior on the part of a few selfish individuals may well take the Northern Terminus away from Baxter and, in my view, that would drastically alter the feeling that hikers get when they reach their goal. The Appalachian Trail, when I attempted it, was pretty much perfect in every way. I'd hate for future generations of hikers to be denied the glory of summiting Katahdin just because some oaf couldn't resist the temptation to have a spliff or take a glug of warm champagne as a bunch of kids hovered nearby.

Having said that, I confess to taking a glug of said beverage when it was handed to me from one of the other hikers at the top. Perhaps my plea for some restraint, on both sides, should be seen from that slightly hypocritical standpoint.

I was aware of none of this controversy when I woke on that final morning; it only erupted on my return, and during 2015. I suspect it will drag on for some time.

Trillium and Jon packed up and headed out at 6:20 a.m., while Tee Bird and I went to find Lighterknot, who was being returned to the park from Millinocket, with Deb and Mama Jean. I was sad that we wouldn't be summiting as a team. We had shared the majority of New Hampshire and Maine together, although I understood Trillium's need to complete the trip with Jon.

It isn't my story to tell, and I certainly won't go into any detail, but Trillium had told us all a couple of weeks before that she had tried to hike the trail in 2012. She had experienced a horrific incident that left her with a reduced lung capacity, along with several other issues that must have plagued her mind since then. The incident took place one evening when she chose to camp just off the trail, by herself. Her return to the A.T. required an enormous amount of courage. It also explained, at least to me, why she was such a hard-headed pain in the ass all the time.

She actually told me the story one day as we were descending an especially difficult rock field. Never being one to let people off with a truncated version of a story, I pressed her for more details about her reaction to the incident. Having gone into the whole story, she then blithely told me that she would do it all over again and that, should the circumstances arise, she would camp by herself once more. I think I called her a bloody idiot at that remark, so we had something of a falling out. Even though things had returned to relative calm between us, I could see why finishing this validating quest was so important to her. Jon, her supportive partner through what must have been very difficult times, was the right person to be with.

There was a signing-in sheet for Katahdin, then Lighterknot, Tee Bird, and I posed for Deb as she took a few photos. We set off up a long, easy incline that eventually took us out of Deb's and Mama Jean's sight. They told us they would be there on our return. Lighterknot kept turning round fully and waving, as if he were a five-year-old on the first day of school. His attachment to both his wife and his mother was touching. I felt that he was lucky that they were there to share his triumph. At one point, Deb had wanted to make the climb, but he had talked her out of it. We had warmed up for over 2,000 miles, while she would have been taking a shot at it cold. Lighterknot had agonized about suggesting that she should stay behind, but it was the right decision for both of them. Deb would have found it extraordinarily difficult, while Lighterknot would have constantly been watching her. It might have impacted the safety of both of their hikes.

The going was comfortable for a mile or so, with the weather cooperating, though it looked cloudy further up the mountain. The trail started to rise gradually and, while it was arduous, with plenty of scrambling up intermittent rocks in our path, it was hardly beyond our capabilities. We made good progress for a couple of miles.

As we got higher, the trees became more sparse, and we emerged above the tree line. Then we hit the rocks. All of a sudden we were into proper climbing, with hand-over-hand stuff that required thinking about. We negotiated our way over steep rocks, and pulled ourselves up using metal bars driven into the boulders at some of the trickiest passages. White blazes would appear in seemingly unattainable spots, even though there was always a way to reach them. It was a kind of vertical Mahoosuc Notch, ever-rising, ever-challenging. New Hampshire had prepared us well for this. I felt in my element, enjoying it hugely while we made our way ever-upwards.

We posed for a few photos, as the clouds were starting to come down and meet us by now. Eventually, we emerged onto the flatter tablelands. The cloud had enveloped us, and we stuck together as the path followed a less strenuous rise. We didn't know precisely where we were, because we couldn't see much more than about 50 yards in any direction. Our excitement was mounting and, even though we heard voices from time to time, the end kept being delayed, with the hill cresting again and again in front of us.

Then I heard a more prolonged chatter and excitement. With just about 75 yards to go, I was able to make out that iconic sign, the sign I'd dreamed of for years, and the sign that had been in my thoughts for much of the past six months. Various hikers were silhouetted at the top, surrounding the sign with an exuberant reverence. I had moved ahead of the other two by this point, although Tee Bird was close behind me, with Lighterknot some way behind her. We had passed Trillium and Jon a short while before.

Drawing nearer, I thought of Diane, and my sons. I was fighting to hold back tears. I had thought of them many times before on this journey—along with everybody else who had played an important part in my life—and I hoped that I had resolved to my own satisfaction the relationships that I wanted to continue to nurture, as well as some I wanted to let go. I had worked out many of my responses to the moral issues of the day, and had even finally rejected the possibility of God.

As I touched the sign to signify the end of my trip, I wish I could say that I felt something deeply meaningful. I

simply felt grateful. I was relieved that it was over and that I hadn't been injured or even worse. I patiently took pictures of Tee Bird on the sign, before I climbed up onto it myself. The relief flooded out of me, and I let go a full-throated roar of achievement and delight. The pictures recorded perfectly what I was feeling in those heady moments.

I then stepped to the side and called Diane and Rob, with both conversations ending in my tears. Diane was delighted for me, but now more eager than ever to see me home. When I confirmed that I'd be back with her within 24 hours, I choked up. Composing myself, I called Rob. He started me off again when he referred to me as Mighty Blue for the very first time. It was a wonderful moment that I will take with me to my grave.

While I was on the phone, I saw Lighterknot approach the sign slowly, then bend and touch it. He offered a silent prayer to God, with whom he has an enduring relationship. I didn't take a picture, but it was another one of the abiding sights that lodged itself in my brain. Trillium and Jon were there as well, and she was silently exorcising her demons at the sign. I was touched at the sight of the two of them together, each understanding what this meant to the other, sharing their emotions in isolation from the rest of us. We even managed a final picture of our band of four that neatly capped off our adventure together.

The descent presented us with similar problems to the ascent. In some ways, it was even tougher to climb down some of the steeper rocks as opposed to up them. However, we were driven by adrenaline and our own thoughts, arriving back safely. It had taken us just over three and a half hours to get to the top, and a similar time to rejoin Deb and Mama Jean.

I could already feel that the band was breaking up, and we were soon to go our separate ways. Having shared such a common purpose, with each other and with others over the entire journey, it felt difficult to say goodbye. In many ways, the separation, when it came, was so quick and final that it was probably for the best. Lighterknot and his family took both Tee Bird and me into Millinocket. They dropped me at the Appalachian Trail Cafe, with quick hugs before moving on to their respective destinations.

I had managed to contact a couple of members of my local Appalachian Trail Club. These were Tim and Vickie Edwards, who had generously offered to run me from this cafe to a hotel near Bangor Airport, in preparation for my return flight the following morning.

Suddenly alone, waiting for Tim and Vickie, I sat quietly with a final burger and looked around me. A sense that I was returning to real life hit me. I knew that my days and nights in the woods were over. There would be no more crummy motels and hostels. I felt calm and satisfied that I now had something extraordinary to help define me. It was also accomplishment that could never be taken away from me. My enthusiasms that had left me with so many incomplete projects had been banished from my psyche. I was no longer haunted by my own disappointment with myself. I truly felt a better person for going on this hike.

Tim and Vickie turned up shortly after and grilled me about the hike on the way to the airport. I'm afraid I was a bit unresponsive. I felt terribly disconnected from them and couldn't understand it. They were hikers and probably understood, so they left me to it.

Some frantic laundry that night allowed me to return home the following morning with a pack of clean clothes when I met Diane at Sarasota airport. She held on to me as we embraced and celebrated my return. As we got in the car, Diane turned and said, with a face that reflected complete disgust, "What on earth is that smell?" before gagging and hastily opening her window. That is actually a truncated version of what she said—the original being considerably more graphic—though it conveys the message.

Unfortunately, I had forgotten to wash my fleece. I hadn't worn it too often in the previous couple of weeks and felt that it wasn't in need of a wash. What I had omitted to take into account was the fact that I had used the fleece as a pillow for about 500 miles. It had become my go-to since I left my actual pillow in a bunch of washing that many miles before. Of course, the gradually accumulated stink had not registered with me. We drove the remainder of the way home with the windows down; not for the first time in the previous six months.

Four months later, I went for another walk. This was more of a local stroll, but it resonated with me so much that it has stuck with me. In the four months since I had completed my hike things hadn't gone as I had expected them to. I had been under the impression that, once I returned home, I'd be able to slip back to my old life without missing a beat. I entirely underestimated the effect the trail had on both my body and my mind.

I knew that it had been physically demanding, yet I also knew that my body had met the various challenges. I had adapted well to each rise and fall in the terrain when I encountered them. Indeed, it was the constant engagement and disengagement of muscles that was the first thing I had noticed physiologically on the trail. That said, I was physically exhausted. It took me about three months before I was able to run up a flight of stairs, while I lost most of my toenails and my feet grew a full shoe size. My knees ached, though that soon eased. The Appalachian Trail is going to examine you physically in a way few things ever can, but it will shred your mind if you let it.

I was aware that I'd shown a mental toughness that some had questioned at the outset. I hadn't doubted myself but, at the same time, I had no idea what I'd face on this trip. It turned out that my apparent strength of purpose was all bluster on my part. Nevertheless, I built the mental toughness as I hiked, so I got there in the end. My mind played tricks with me. I could feel glum and I could feel content, though I was often not able to identify between the two. My emotions were strung out the whole time by the confluence of my past and the time I had to think about it. Allowing that to happen let me face—and at least own up to—who I was.

My local stroll around the neighborhood could not have been less like the Appalachian Trail. For a start, there were no roots ready to pull down the unsuspecting traveler, nor were there rocks to either climb or slip on. I should also record that the very topography of Florida leaves out those pesky mountains that get in the way from time to time on the A.T. Lastly, there appeared to be no animals out to eat me, which is always a bit of a bonus on a walk.

As I reflected further, I realized that the feeling of being disconnected I'd felt with Tim and Vickie Edwards had remained with me. Nothing in my life had been how it was in the woods. Nothing in the woods had been how my life had felt before. My very roots had been pulled from me by the hike. I felt vulnerable for probably the first time in my life. My thoughts were constantly churning in my head, and I found my previous focus to be utterly missing.

Being retired, I would find myself walking around the house in an apparent need to do something, though achieving hardly anything all day. I even suspected I might be depressed. In fact, when I broached this subject with an old friend, a Vietnam veteran, he said it might be some form of PTSD. "Minus the part with the Vietcong shooting at me," I immediately commented.

Since I've returned home—to a considerably more sedentary lifestyle—my wife has regularly remarked that I'm far too hard on myself. I've never been this way before, with neither self-doubt nor self-recrimination clouding my day. I have pinpointed my hike as the start of this new, slightly bemusing habit. It is certainly one of the more negative things I've taken from this experience. I now find it more difficult to give myself a pass for things not done.

Diane says that I ignore the many good things that I do during the day, and only get crazy about the things I don't do. Some might say that this is a positive development, but I don't cope with it well. It is certainly a lasting legacy of my hike and one that I am constantly battling against. I really can't wait to get back to no self-recrimination; life was far easier with that as part of my makeup.

I vowed never to hike again, and had even included that comment in a number of presentations I did locally, much to my audiences' doubt and amusement. Despite that, the woods rarely left my thoughts. Lighterknot and Tee Bird started talking about doing the John Muir Trail in 2016. I wasn't in the least bit interested. One day I watched a film on Netflix with Diane, called *Mile... Mile & a Half*. It was a documentary about the JMT. As I was watching, I turned to see Diane looking intently at me. "You want to do it, don't you?" she asked. I hadn't realized it, but, yes, I did want to do it. Diane has long been a proponent of living your best life, and, particularly given her own curtailed circumstances, she encouraged me to join the other two. The three of us, along with Tee Bird's husband, are scheduled to start the hike in early July 2016.

As for the rest of it, I have stepped up my involvement in the Family Partnership Center and become far more charitable in my thinking. Carrying everything on my back allowed me to understand how little I needed, giving me a greater awareness of those who actually have nothing and heightening my empathy for their plight. It is hard to believe that there is such poverty in the richest country in the world, but it is there, folks; you just need to open your eyes to it, and it will be all around you.

Once I'd realized how out of focus I had become, I started to discipline myself to write my story, although that, too, seemed to share characteristics with the hike. Lots of time alone, in your own head, and quite a marathon to complete. Now, over a year down the line, some of my focus has returned. I enjoy reflecting upon my adventure in a way that I wasn't able to in its immediate aftermath. I'm still sometimes concerned at the thoughts running around in my head, but I wouldn't change a thing.

I've had the opportunity to think about those I met on the trail and especially the friends who came to visit me. In retrospect, I've looked back on the achievement and see what they all saw then. Hiking the Appalachian Trail is something extraordinary, but something that can be achieved by anybody if he or she is prepared to commit fully to the task.

Diane allowed me the space to work out what I wanted to do in my life and I think we were both taken aback at the change in me. Yet, this is now me. I like myself a whole lot more than I did. I've come to terms with many of my mistakes and bad behavior in my life, and I've assumed a resilience I hadn't previously suspected. I've also ruled out any possibility of the existence of God. This has, perhaps counter-intuitively, allowed me to gain control of my life and my own happiness. I have a moral code that isn't centered around somebody else's idea of what is right and wrong. My code was handed down to me by my parents. Now that I am no longer constantly anesthetized by alcohol, I pay a lot more attention to that code. All in all, I'm okay with the person I became.

Who'd have thought that my own Appalachian Trial would provide me with such a diversity of riches, yet turn my life upside down? I had to walk nearly 2,200 miles to discover who I was. I wonder what your Appalachian Trial will give you?

My Appalachian Trial II: Creaking Geezer, Hidden Flagon

A Call to Action

Thanks so much for reading *My Appalachian Trial II: Creaking Geezer, Hidden Flagon*. I really hope that you enjoyed it. Before you go, I wonder if you could do me a favor and leave a review for me on the Amazon website? It really won't take you long and it would mean so very much to me.

Thanks very much.

Continue the Journey

If you enjoyed this concluding volume of my book, then I hope you've read the first one, *My Appalachian Trial I—Three Weddings and a Sabbatical*. This book tells of my dream to hike the trail, my often misguided preparations, and my tentative first steps. You'll be laughing, both with and at me, while you share some of my reflections on the trail and on life.

If you would like to read more, please turn the page and get a free bonus.

One last thing

Now that I've completed my journey, I've been writing yet another book on the Appalachian Trail. This one is called *Hiking the Appalachian Trail is Easy: Especially if You've Never Hiked Before*. The good news about this book is that it is going to be the best possible price—FREE!!!

To reserve your copy, please visit my website www.steveadams.info/contact and sign up for my email list. As soon as the book is available, you will get an email with a link that will allow you to download it.

Made in the
USA
Columbia, SC